AF116565

SAVAISM

JUDAH EVAN MILLER

SAVAISM

Copyright © 2024 by Judah Evan Miller
All rights reserved. No part of this book may be reproduced in any manner whatsoever without written permission except in the case of brief quotations embodied in critical articles and reviews.
First Printing, 2024

Contents

1 Introduction 1
2 A Broken Economy 12
3 A Better Way 70
4 Practicality 123

1

Introduction

Sava: Economic abundance signifying material fullness and profound contentment.

Introduction to Savaism: A New Economic Model for a Changing World

In 1950, the median home price in the United States was about $7,354, while the median household income was approximately $2,990. This gives a price-to-income ratio of about 2.5, meaning a typical home cost around 2.5 times the annual household income. As of 2024, the median home price has risen to $416,100, and the median household income is about $74,580, resulting in a price-to-income ratio of 5.6. This indicates that it is now more than twice as difficult to afford a home compared to 1950. Since 1950, the U.S. Gross Domestic Product (GDP) has grown dramatically. In 1950, the nominal GDP was approximately $300 billion. By

2023, it had risen to about $27.36 trillion, reflecting an increase of over 90-fold in nominal terms. There is definitively more to go around yet there substantially less in the hands of the people. Where did it go? Who has it? And how can we get it back. That's what this book aims to find out.

In today's world, the debate around economic systems seems to be stuck in an endless loop, with capitalism and socialism dominating the conversation. On one side, capitalism is lauded for promoting innovation, competition, and individual freedom, yet it's also criticized for fostering inequality, environmental degradation, and a focus on profit over people. On the other side, socialism is praised for its emphasis on equality, collective welfare, and the redistribution of resources, but it's also condemned for stifling innovation, curbing personal freedoms, and leading to inefficient economies. Both systems, though fundamentally different, share a common flaw: they fail to address the root causes of economic inequity and sustainability.

Why Savaism?

Savaism offers a fresh perspective a third way that isn't constrained by the binary choice between capitalism and socialism. It's built on the simple yet profound idea that there's enough wealth in the world to ensure everyone's basic needs are met without the need for aggressive government intervention or corporate dominance. The term "Savaism" derives from the word Sava, symbolizing abundance and contentment. It represents an economic philosophy centered on the belief that prosperity can be achieved without sacrificing fairness or freedom.

In essence, Savaism is about creating an economic environment where wealth doesn't just trickle down from the top or get forcefully redistributed from the rich to the poor. Instead, it's about ensuring that the systems in place prevent wealth from being hoarded in the first place. Savaism aims to build a society where resources are abundant and accessible to all, where economic policies foster inclusivity, and where businesses thrive by contributing to the well-being of society as a whole rather than solely focusing on profits.

The Limitations of Capitalism and Socialism

To understand why Savaism is needed, it's crucial to first acknowledge the limitations of the current dominant economic systems. Capitalism, with its emphasis on free markets and individual success, has undoubtedly driven technological advancements and lifted millions out of poverty. However, it has also led to significant disparities in wealth and power. In many capitalist economies, a small percentage of the population controls a vast majority of the wealth, while many struggle to make ends meet. This concentration of wealth often results in an imbalance of power, where the wealthy exert disproportionate influence over political and economic decisions, perpetuating a cycle of inequality.

On the other hand, socialism seeks to address inequality by advocating for the redistribution of wealth through government intervention. The idea is that by taxing the wealthy and providing social services, everyone can achieve a basic standard of living. However, this approach often comes at a cost. This is why the term wealth redistribution is always framed in a passive tense, because wealth redistributing raises the questions, "Who is doing the redistributing?" And "Who has that power?" When the government assumes the power to control wealth distribution, it can lead to inefficiencies and stifle innovation, as competition diminishes. More critically, heavy government involvement in the economy frequently results in a significant loss of personal freedoms, as individuals lose the ability to make independent decisions about their own economic lives, placing control in the hands of the state.

Both systems have their strengths and weaknesses, but neither provides a holistic solution to the challenges of modern economies. They represent two extremes one that prioritizes individual success at the expense of societal welfare, and another that focuses on collective welfare but often at the cost of economic efficiency and personal freedom.

The Core Principles of Savaism

Savaism seeks to bridge the gap between these two extremes by focusing on three core principles: fairness, freedom, and sustainability. These principles are not just theoretical; they are the foundation upon which practical policies and economic structures can be built.

1. Fairness: In a Savaist economy, fairness is about more than just equal distribution of wealth; it's about creating opportunities for all individuals to succeed. This means ensuring that everyone has access to education, healthcare, and other essential services, and that these services are provided in a way that empowers individuals rather than creating dependency. Fairness also involves preventing the accumulation of excessive wealth and power by a few, which often leads to corruption and inequality.

2. Freedom: Savaism values personal freedom, recognizing that individuals should have the autonomy to make choices about their own lives. This includes the freedom to pursue economic opportunities, to start businesses, and to innovate. However, this freedom is balanced with the need to ensure that one person's freedom does not come at the expense of others. In a Savaist system, regulations are designed to prevent exploitation and to protect the environment and public welfare, without stifling creativity and entrepreneurship.

3. Sustainability: Economic policies under Savaism are designed with long-term sustainability in mind. This means not only environmental sustainability but also economic and social sustainability. A Savaist economy would focus on creating jobs that contribute to the well-being of society, on businesses that operate responsibly, and on policies that ensure future generations can thrive. Sustainability also means avoiding the boom-and-bust cycles that plague capitalist economies by fostering stable, inclusive growth.

Preventing Wealth Hoarding

One of the key issues Savaism addresses is the hoarding of wealth by a small elite. In both capitalist and socialist systems, wealth tends to accumulate at the top, either through the market mechanisms of capitalism or the bureaucratic structures of socialism. Savaism proposes a different approach, where the focus is on preventing this accumulation from happening in the first place.

This is achieved through a combination of policies that encourage wealth to be reinvested in the economy, rather than being hoarded. For example, instead of heavy taxes on income or wealth, Savaism might advocate for incentives that encourage businesses to reinvest their profits in local communities, in their employees, or in sustainable practices. The goal is to create a virtuous cycle where wealth is continuously circulated through the economy, benefiting everyone rather than being concentrated in the hands of a few.

The Role of Government and Corporations in Savaism

In a Savaist economy, the role of government is to set the rules of the game and ensure they are followed. This doesn't mean heavy-handed regulation or control, but rather a framework that encourages fair competition, innovation, and sustainability. The government's role is to prevent monopolies, to protect workers' rights, and to ensure that businesses operate in a way that benefits society as a whole.

Corporations, on the other hand, are seen as partners in building a prosperous society. In a Savaist economy, businesses are encouraged to pursue profits, but not at the expense of the environment, workers, or the broader community. Companies that prioritize sustainability, fair wages, and ethical practices are rewarded, not just by the government incentives but also by the market itself.

Savaism is an economic philosophy that rejects the conventional dichotomy between socialism and corporatism. Instead of focusing on wealth redistribution through government intervention, Savaism emphasizes the importance of incentivizing the wealthy to reinvest their capital back into society rather than hoarding it. The core idea is that economic prosperity can be achieved without the need for the state to forcibly redistribute wealth from the rich to the poor. By encouraging reinvestment, Savaism aims to create a more equitable economy where wealth naturally circulates, benefiting all levels of society. This approach seeks to ensure that wealth flows back into productive uses, fostering innovation, job creation, and overall economic growth, rather than being concentrated in the hands of a few elites.

The Need for a New Economic Model

The world is changing rapidly, and the economic models of the past are struggling to keep up. Globalization, technological advancements, and environmental challenges are creating new dynamics that the traditional systems of capitalism and socialism are ill-equipped to handle. In this context, Savaism offers a new way forward one that combines the best aspects of both systems while avoiding their pitfalls.

Savaism is not about tearing down the existing economic order but about building a new one that works for everyone. It's about recognizing that there is enough wealth in the world to go around, and that the key to a prosperous society is not in accumulating wealth but in ensuring it is used wisely and distributed fairly without being unfairly torn out of the hands of citizens. It's about creating an economy that is both dynamic and inclusive, where innovation is encouraged, but not at the expense of social welfare.

A Call to Action

As we move forward, it's important to recognize that the challenges we face are complex and multifaceted. There is no one-size-fits-all solution, and Savaism does not pretend to offer all the answers. However, it does provide a framework for thinking differently about our economy one that prioritizes fairness, freedom, and sustainability. It's a call to rethink the way we approach economic policy, to move beyond the outdated debates of capitalism versus socialism, and to embrace a new model that works for everyone. It's not about wealth redistribution. It's about incentivizing the reinvestment of wealth rather than the Hoarding of the elite.

Savaism is not just an economic theory; it's a vision for the future. It's a vision of a world where prosperity is shared, where businesses thrive by doing good, and where individuals are empowered to achieve their full potential. It's a vision of an economy that serves the people, not the other way around.

In the chapters that follow, we will explore in more detail the problems with the current economic models, the principles of Savaism, and how this new model can be implemented in the real world. We will look at practical examples and case studies, and we will discuss the potential benefits of embracing this new way of thinking. But most importantly, we will make the case that Savaism is not just an alternative it is a necessary evolution of our economic systems if we are to build a more just, sustainable, and prosperous world for future generations.

Sources for chapter:

USAFacts. (n.d.). Gross domestic product (GDP). USAFacts. Retrieved August 29, 2024, from https://usafacts.org/data/topics/economy/economic-indicators/gdp/gross-domestic-product/

Federal Reserve Bank of St. Louis. (n.d.). Nominal gross domestic product for United States [NGDPXDCUSA]. FRED, Federal Reserve Bank of St. Louis. Retrieved August 29, 2024, from https://fred.stlouisfed.org/series/NGDPXDCUSA

Orchard. (2022, December 6). How much the average home cost in your state in 1950. Orchard. Retrieved August 29, 2024, from https://orchard.com/blog/posts/how-much-the-typical-home-cost-in-your-state-in-1950

Better Mortgage. (2020, July 1). Here's how much home prices have risen since 1950. Better Mortgage. Retrieved August 29, 2024, from https://better.com/content/how-much-home-prices-have-risen-since-1950

Wallach, O. (2024, February 27). Charted: U.S. median house prices vs. income. Visual Capitalist. Retrieved August 29, 2024, from https://www.visualcapitalist.com/median-house-prices-vs-income-us/

2

A Broken Economy

Definitions:

Corporatism: the organization of a society into industrial and professional corporations serving as organs of political representation and exercising control over persons and activities within their jurisdiction

Crony Capitalism: An economic system characterized by close, mutually advantageous relationships between business leaders and government officials.

Capitalism: An economic system in which investment in and ownership of the means of production, distribution, and exchange of wealth is made and maintained chiefly by private individuals or corporations, especially as contrasted to cooperatively or state-owned means of wealth.

Socialism: A theory or system of social organization in which the means of production, distribution, and exchange are owned or regulated by the community as a whole, typically through a centralized government.

Communism: A political and economic ideology advocating for a classless system in which the means of production are owned communally, and private property is non-existent or severely curtailed.

All definitions sourced by Merriam-Webster Dictionary.

Practical functionality:

- Socialism: the power of wealth distribution being in the hands of a large government.
- Extreme: The government decides where you work, where you shop and how much you get paid.

- Corporatism: the power of wealth disruption being in the hands of large companies.
- Extreme: Corporations decide where you work, where you shop and how much you get paid.

- Communism: the power of resource distribution in the hands of a large government.

- Capitalism: the power of wealth being in the hands of the markets/no one.

The far right shouts in favor of big corporations and small government. The far left shouts in favor of big government and small corporations, but what this book aims to prove is the similarities between them. Along with the end result. They both lead to the same thing, a large entity controlling the wealth. This kind of governance always leads to the same problems. Problems that become highly evident but remain difficult to diagnose. This chapter hopes to provide a better understanding of the pressing issues facing our broken economy.

Problems:

Problem 1: Capitalism always leads to corporatism.

Over the last decade or so, the narrative has shifted. The general population often cannot distinguish between corporatism and capitalism. The government and major news platforms may teach that they are one and the same, but in reality, they couldn't be more different. Mussolini famously said, "Fascism should more appropriately be called corporatism because it is a merger of state and corporate power." Corporatism and socialism, in some ways, are closely related. Capitalism, on the other hand, is a free market system where control is in the hands of the people. However, corporatism and capitalism do share one thing in common: unchecked capitalism often evolves into corporatism. Thus, capitalism, when left unregulated, cannot truly exist because, when no one governs wealth, a power vacuum forms.Problem 2: Wealth inequality

To the more conservative readers, don't put the book down yet. Let me explain. The gdp has only gone up and it has grown relative to population as well. There is definitively more to go around so why is there less in the pockets of the people? Wealth inequality.

Wealth inequality has increasingly become a pressing concern in many societies, and it is often intertwined with its variant, crony capitalism. At the heart of crony capitalism is the idea that wealth and power are concentrated among a select few, often due to close relationships between business leaders and government officials rather than merit, competition, or democratic choice. This intertwining of business and government can exacerbate wealth inequality for several reasons:

1. Distorted Market Competition: In a crony capitalist system, government policies, regulations, and contracts are often designed to favor certain businesses over others. This distortion can stifle competition, as companies with political connections are more likely to succeed than those based solely on the quality of their products or services. As a result, wealth accumulates in the hands of a few, undermining the equality principles of market competition and meritocracy.

2. Barrier to Entry: Crony capitalism raises significant barriers to entry for new businesses. When political connections are a prerequisite for success, entrepreneurs without these connections are disadvantaged. This limitation on new entrants not only reduces innovation but also concentrates wealth among established businesses and their political allies.

3. Resource Allocation: Government resources, which could be used to address social issues or promote equitable economic growth, may instead be allocated to projects that benefit a few individuals or companies. This misallocation

can lead to underinvestment in public goods like education, healthcare, and infrastructure, which are crucial for reducing wealth inequality.

4. Public Trust and Social Cohesion: The perception that wealth and success are the results of unfair advantages rather than hard work and talent can erode public trust in both the economic and political systems. This erosion of trust can lead to social unrest and decreased social cohesion, as the population becomes increasingly divided between the wealthy elite and those left behind.

Addressing the issues of wealth inequality and crony capitalism requires comprehensive reforms that ensure transparency, promote fair competition, and dismantle the undue influence of wealth in politics. Policies might include campaign finance reform, stricter enforcement of antitrust laws, and the implementation of measures to increase government transparency and accountability. Additionally, promoting equal access to education and opportunities for entrepreneurship can help level the playing field.

Problem 3: Artificial inflation

The phenomenon of artificial inflation within the real estate market, notably influenced by significant Wall Street investments, encapsulates a pressing issue with far-reaching socioeconomic implications. This trend, wherein large financial entities and investment firms acquire substantial portfolios of residential properties, not only distorts housing prices but also fundamentally alters the fabric of communities and the accessibility of homeownership for the average individual.

Driving Prices Beyond Reach

Wall Street's foray into the real estate market has led to an artificial inflation of housing prices. By purchasing homes en masse, often with the advantage of cash offers well above market rates, these entities create upward pressure on prices, making homeownership increasingly unattainable for individual buyers and families. This situation exacerbates housing affordability crises in many areas, pushing the dream of homeownership out of reach for the middle and working classes and contributing to a growing wealth gap.

The Transformation of Neighborhoods

The significant presence of institutional investors in residential real estate markets has transformative effects on neighborhoods. With a focus on maximizing returns, these investors may prioritize short-term profits over long-term community development, leading to underinvestment in property maintenance and a decline in the quality of living conditions. Additionally, the shift from homeowner-occupied to investor-owned properties can erode the sense of community and stability that is foundational to vibrant neighborhoods, as transient tenant populations replace long-term residents.

Barriers to Entry for First-Time Homebuyers

The competitive edge that institutional investors hold in the real estate market, including the ability to make all-cash offers and close deals quickly, places first-time and individual homebuyers at a significant disadvantage. This dynamic can lead to a discouraging environment for potential homeowners, where bidding wars against financially robust entities become the norm, further complicating the path to homeownership for many.

Exacerbation of Rental Market Pressures

As Wall Street firms convert purchased properties into rental units to generate ongoing income, the dynamics of the rental market are also affected. The reduction in available homes for purchase increases demand in the rental market, driving up rent prices and placing additional financial strain on individuals and families who are already priced out of homeownership. This cycle of rising rents and housing costs contributes to economic instability and increases the burden on social safety nets.

The involvement of Wall Street in the real estate sector, through the artificial inflation of housing prices and the consequent socioeconomic ramifications, underscores a critical area of concern. This trend not only challenges the traditional pathways to homeownership and financial stability for many but also raises questions about the long-term sustainability of such investment practices. Addressing these issues requires a nuanced understanding of the interplay between large-scale investment activities and their impacts on the real estate market, alongside policies aimed at ensuring the housing market serves the broader public interest, promoting equitable access to homeownership, and preserving community integrity.

Summary

Artificial inflation in housing markets is a deliberate tactic used by wealthy investors and corporations to manipulate property values, making homeownership increasingly unattainable for ordinary people. These entities buy large quantities of properties in desirable areas, reducing the available supply and driving up prices through artificially created demand. This allows them to sell at higher prices or rent at inflated rates, while ordinary buyers face escalating costs for basic housing. As prices rise, so do rents, trapping many in a cycle of unaffordability and deepening economic inequality.

A key tool in this manipulation is the use of real estate comparables, or "comps," which determine market values based on recent sales. By inflating these comps, investors set a higher baseline for property prices, further driving up costs in the area. This cyclical effect allows them to continually push values higher, making it nearly impossible for regular buyers to compete. This greed-driven practice creates significant economic and social imbalances, undermining the stability and fairness of housing markets and leaving many people unable to achieve the dream of homeownership.

Problem 4: Unaffordable Healthcare

The healthcare crisis in the United States is often painted as a choice between two extremes: either individuals bear the burden of exorbitant medical bills, or the government steps in to cover these costs. However, this framing overlooks a critical question: why are these healthcare bills so high in the first place?

The root of the issue lies in what can be described as a healthcare cartel, driven by Wall Street greed. The healthcare industry, including hospitals, insurance companies, and even pharmaceutical firms, has become deeply intertwined through mutual stock ownership and investments. This consolidation creates a significant conflict of interest. Instead of focusing on patient care, these entities prioritize profit maximization, often at the expense of the public's health and financial stability.

In a fair and functional system, health insurance should serve as a buffer between individuals and catastrophic healthcare costs. A person pays premiums to an insurance company, and in return, the insurance company should cover their medical expenses when needed. This model is supposed to protect individuals from financial ruin due to unexpected health issues.

However, the reality is starkly different. Insurance companies and healthcare providers have developed a symbiotic relationship that benefits both, while harming consumers. Here's how it works:

1. Inflated Prices: Insurance companies encourage hospitals and doctors to inflate their prices to levels that no ordinary person could afford. This artificially high pricing forces everyone to rely on health insurance.

2. Discounts for Insurers: After the prices are inflated, hospitals give substantial discounts to insurance companies, bringing the actual cost down to more reasonable levels—often close to what the original price would have been without the inflation.

3. False Appearances: The insurance companies then claim to be paying off these exorbitant bills on behalf of their customers, but in reality, they are paying much less. This gives the illusion that they are providing a valuable service when, in fact, they are colluding with healthcare providers to maintain high prices and increase their profits.

4. Profit from the Uninsured: Those without insurance are hit the hardest. They are charged the full inflated prices, which can lead to financial ruin. Meanwhile, both hospitals and insurance companies profit immensely from this system, with billions of dollars flowing into the pockets of a select few on Wall Street.

This setup creates a "win-win" situation for healthcare providers and insurers, while the general public loses. The proposed solution of having the government foot the bill for these inflated costs doesn't solve the underlying problem—it simply shifts the burden from individuals to taxpayers. This would only perpetuate the cycle of greed and inefficiency, as government payments would continue to feed the profits of these conglomerates without addressing the root causes of high healthcare costs.

Sources for section

1. Rosenthal, E. (2017). An American sickness: How healthcare became big business and how you can take it back. Penguin Press.

2. Brill, S. (2015). America's bitter pill: Money, politics, backroom deals, and the fight to fix our broken healthcare system. Random House.

Problem 5: Unaffordable Education

Education tends to have the same problems except in place of insurance companies incentivizing higher prices you have banks who stand to profit from student loans. And you see more of the same problematic solutions. The government's big solution is fronting that cost, which either burdens the tax payer or causes inflation.

The following information is a quote by Tom Stagliano
"Let's do the math.
There 6,700 undergraduates at Harvard.
The tuition for one year of Harvard is currently $45,000, But let us call it $50,000.
Therefore, Harvard would collect $335 Million per year in tuition.
The current Harvard endowment is $37 Billion. If one percent of that endowment (and the endowment usually Grows at 5% or better per year) is used to defray tuition that is: 1% of $37 Billion is $370 Million.
$370 million is generally more than $335 million......
That is why Harvard is need-blind for all undergraduate admissions and promises up to full financial aid for the economically disadvantaged. However, those undergraduates who can afford to pay the full amount will pay the full amount. Harvard offers No merit scholarships and No athletic scholarships.
And the endowment continues to Grow."

It's been reported that Harvard University's endowment is so large that it could cover the entire cost of tuition for all its students for over 200 years. In the time between that quote above and the writing of this book the endowment has gone up. Harvard's endowment, now valued at over $50 billion, is the largest of any academic institution in the world. With the annual distribution from the endowment being a significant source of revenue—about 37% of the university's operating income—Harvard could theoretically use this wealth to fund tuition indefinitely.

This idea proves true for more than just Harvard.

Here is a list of some colleges and universities with their endowment sizes:

1. Harvard University: $50.9 billion
2. Yale University: $42.3 billion
3. Stanford University: $37.8 billion
4. Princeton University: $37.7 billion
5. Massachusetts Institute of Technology (MIT): $27.4 billion
6. University of Pennsylvania: $20.7 billion
7. University of Notre Dame: $16.7 billion
8. Duke University: $12.1 billion
9. Northwestern University: $14.1 billion
10. University of Michigan: $17.3 billion
11. Columbia University: $13.3 billion
12. University of California, Los Angeles (UCLA): $5.1 billion
13. Brown University: $6.1 billion

14. Vanderbilt University: $10.2 billion
15. Rice University: $7.8 billion
16. Emory University: $10 billion
17. Washington University in St. Louis: $12.3 billion
18. University of Southern California (USC): $8.3 billion
19. Carnegie Mellon University: $3.9 billion
20. University of Virginia: $9.9 billion

In light of these staggering endowment figures, it's clear that many of the nation's universities are sitting on immense wealth, wealth that could easily cover tuition costs and beyond without requiring a single additional dollar from students or taxpayers. Yet, instead of leveraging these resources to alleviate the financial burden on students, these institutions continue to rely heavily on tuition, student loans, and government aid. This is a prime example of the broader systemic issue: wealth is often hoarded at the top rather than reinvested in ways that benefit society as a whole. Savaism challenges this status quo by advocating for a system where wealth is actively reinvested, ensuring that educational institutions fulfill their potential as engines of opportunity rather than gateways to debt.

Sources for section:

Harvard University. (2023). Harvard's endowment. Harvard Financial Administration. Retrieved from https://finance.harvard.edu/endowment

Harvard University. (2022). Harvard reports $406-million surplus, but endowment declines. Harvard Magazine. Retrieved from https://www.harvardmagazine.com/2022/10/harvard-endowment-surplus-2022

Stein, J., Campbell, J., & Wu, A. (2023). Economic budgeting for endowment-dependent universities. Harvard Law School Forum on Corporate Governance. Retrieved from https://corpgov.law.harvard.edu/2023/07/30/economic-budgeting-for-endowment-dependent-universities/

National Center for Education Statistics. (2024). Fast facts: College and university endowments. Retrieved from https://nces.ed.gov/fastfacts/display.asp?id=73

Inside Higher Ed. (2024). Endowments per full-time-equivalent student. Retrieved from https://www.insidehighered.com/news/2024/08/28/endowment-data

Commonfund. (2024). A closer look at community colleges. Retrieved from https://www.commonfund.org/news/a-closer-look-at-community-colleges

Problem 6: The Federal Reserve

Centralized federal banks, often referred to as central banks, have been both praised and criticized for their role in managing a country's monetary policy and banking system. While they provide stability and can mitigate economic crises, they also face criticism for several reasons:

1. Lack of Accountability: Central banks are often independent institutions, which can insulate them from direct political influence. However, this independence can also lead to a lack of accountability to the public. Decisions made by central banks, such as interest rate changes or quantitative easing programs, can have significant impacts on the economy, yet the public may have limited input or oversight into these decisions.

2. Inequality: Monetary policies implemented by central banks can exacerbate wealth inequality. For example, policies like quantitative easing, which involves purchasing government securities to inject liquidity into the financial system, have been criticized for primarily benefiting asset holders such as wealthy investors and corporations, rather than average citizens. This can widen the wealth gap between the rich and the poor.

3. Economic Distortions: Centralized control over monetary policy can lead to economic distortions. For instance, artificially low interest rates set by central banks can encourage excessive borrowing and risk-taking behavior,

which may fuel asset bubbles in housing or stock markets. When these bubbles burst, they can result in severe economic downturns, as seen in the 2008 financial crisis.

4. Manipulation of Currency: Central banks have the power to manipulate their country's currency through actions like foreign exchange interventions or adjustments to interest rates. While these interventions can stabilize currency values and promote export competitiveness, they can also be used for political purposes or to gain unfair trade advantages, leading to tensions between nations.

5. Inflationary Pressures: Critics argue that central banks' expansionary monetary policies, such as increasing the money supply or keeping interest rates low for extended periods, can lead to inflationary pressures. This can erode the purchasing power of consumers' savings and wages, particularly for those on fixed incomes or with limited assets to hedge against inflation.

6. Moral Hazard: Central banks' interventions to bail out troubled financial institutions during crises can create moral hazard by incentivizing excessive risk-taking behavior. Knowing that central banks stand ready to provide liquidity or rescue failing banks can encourage banks and other financial entities to engage in risky practices, confident that they will be shielded from the full consequences of their actions.

The Federal Reserve Founding

Historical Opposition: Lincoln, JFK, and Andrew Jackson

- Abraham Lincoln: During the American Civil War, President Abraham Lincoln sought ways to finance the Union's war effort without relying on private banks, which he believed could exert too much control over national finances. To avoid borrowing from these banks at high interest rates, Lincoln issued government-backed currency known as "Greenbacks" under the Legal Tender Act of 1862. This move was part of his broader resistance to centralized banking power, a stance that reflected his concerns over private financial control of national currencies.

- John F. Kennedy: President John F. Kennedy's administration made significant moves toward altering the financial system, notably through Executive Order 11110, signed on June 4, 1963. This order authorized the U.S. Treasury to issue Silver Certificates, which were backed by silver held by the government. This action was seen as an effort to reduce the Federal Reserve's control over currency issuance by allowing the Treasury to create money independently of the central banking system. Kennedy's monetary policy decisions are often viewed as part of a broader attempt to challenge the Federal Reserve's dominance over U.S. currency .

- Andrew Jackson: Perhaps the most notable historical figure in the fight against centralized banking was President

Andrew Jackson. He fiercely opposed the Second Bank of the United States, which operated similarly to a central bank. Jackson believed it was unconstitutional and dangerous to the republic because it concentrated financial power in the hands of a few elites. He successfully vetoed the recharter of the Bank in 1832 and ultimately succeeded in dismantling it by 1836. Jackson's opposition to centralized banking is a foundational moment in American history, and the establishment of the Federal Reserve in 1913, the same year Jackson died, is often seen as a turning point in the return of centralized financial control.

The Secretive Founding of the Federal Reserve
- The Federal Reserve Act was passed on December 23, 1913, in a highly unusual session of Congress. The vote occurred late at night after many lawmakers had already left Washington, D.C., for the Christmas holiday. According to historical records, only a few members of Congress were present during the vote, leading to its passage with little opposition. This method of passing the legislation, especially for something as significant as establishing a central bank, has been heavily scrutinized and criticized over the years. The lack of transparency and the timing of the vote have raised questions about the process, suggesting that the act was pushed through under circumstances designed to avoid public and legislative scrutiny .

Private Ownership

- The Federal Reserve, while technically a private institution, operates as the central bank of the United States. Its ownership and structure have been subjects of extensive analysis. The Federal Reserve System is composed of 12 regional Federal Reserve Banks, which are owned by private member banks within their respective districts. These member banks, in turn, are privately owned. The influence of powerful banking families is frequently noted in discussions of the Federal Reserve's establishment and operations. While the Federal Reserve is governed by a Board of Governors appointed by the U.S. President and confirmed by the Senate, its operational independence and the private ownership of its regional banks contribute to ongoing discussions about the extent of private control within the system.

The Federal Reserve's Control Over Money

- The Federal Reserve holds considerable power over the U.S. economy through its control of the money supply, interest rates, and its role as a lender of last resort. The U.S. dollar (USD), issued and managed by the Federal Reserve, is the world's reserve currency, meaning it is used as the primary currency for international trade and finance. This status gives the Federal Reserve significant influence over global economic conditions. The institution's ability to create money, influence credit, and control inflation rates gives it unparalleled authority in both national and international economic matters. The Federal Reserve's structure as a privately controlled but publicly overseen entity has sparked debates about the concentration of economic power and the potential for conflicts of interest between private banking interests and public welfare.

Summary

The Federal Reserve, established in 1913, remains one of the most powerful financial institutions in the world. Its creation marked a significant shift in U.S. monetary policy, centralizing control over the nation's money supply in a semi-private institution. Historical figures such as Abraham Lincoln, John F. Kennedy, and Andrew Jackson all recognized the dangers of centralized banking power, and their efforts to limit or reform such power are key moments in U.S. history.

The circumstances surrounding the Federal Reserve's founding, its operational structure, and the involvement of private banking interests continue to be areas of significant interest and discussion. The Federal Reserve's control over the issuance of the U.S. dollar, the world's reserve currency, underscores its global influence and the importance of understanding its role in both national and international financial systems.

In conclusion, while centralized federal banks play a crucial role in stabilizing economies and managing monetary policy, they are not without their drawbacks. Critics argue that their lack of accountability, potential to exacerbate inequality, and tendency for economic distortions raise concerns about their effectiveness and long-term sustainability.

Balancing the need for stability with the risks associated with centralized control remains a key challenge for policymakers and central bankers worldwide.

Sources for section:

1. - (https://www.thelincolnfinancialfoundation.org): Lincoln Financial Foundation, analysis of Lincoln's monetary policies during the Civil War.
2. - (https://www.archives.gov): National Archives, detailing Executive Orders and their implications.
3. - (https://www.jfklibrary.org): JFK Library, documentation of Kennedy's Executive Orders and financial policies.
4. - (https://www.loc.gov): Library of Congress, records of Andrew Jackson's presidency and the Bank War.
5. - (https://www.history.com): History.com, articles on Andrew Jackson's battle against the Second Bank of the United States.
6. - (https://www.federalreservehistory.org): Federal Reserve History, the official narrative of the Federal Reserve's founding.
7. - (https://www.senate.gov): U.S. Senate historical records, analysis of the passage of the Federal Reserve Act.
8. - (https://www.britannica.com): Encyclopaedia Britannica, discussion of the Federal Reserve System and its ownership.
9. - (https://www.investopedia.com): Investopedia, explaining the structure and ownership of the Federal Reserve.

10. - (https://www.federalreserve.gov): Federal Reserve's official website, outlining its role in the U.S. and global economy.
11. - (https://www.imf.org): International Monetary Fund, articles on the U.S. dollar as the world's reserve currency.

Problem 7: The Dominance of Wall Street

The influence of Wall Street on the market and the broader economy, while complex and multifaceted, has caused numerous negative repercussions, eventuating systemic issues within its operation. This critique delves into the darker facets of Wall Street's operations, shedding light on the detrimental impacts these practices have on economic stability, corporate governance, and societal equity.

Short-Termism and Market Volatility

Wall Street's relentless focus on short-term performance, often measured in quarterly earnings, perpetuates a cycle of market volatility and near sighted corporate strategies. This short-termism pressures companies to prioritize immediate financial results over long-term sustainability and growth. Such an environment discourages investments in innovation, employee development, and infrastructure, which are vital for sustained economic health but may not yield immediate financial returns. The resultant market volatility not only makes the financial system more susceptible to shocks but also erodes public confidence in investment as a vehicle for long-term savings and retirement planning.

Distortion of Corporate Priorities

The disproportionate emphasis on stock prices and shareholder returns can distort corporate priorities, leading to practices that undermine the broader economic and societal interests. For example, stock buybacks a practice used to artificially inflate share prices divert funds away from potential investments in wages, job creation, or research and development. Moreover, executive compensation packages heavily tied to stock performance can incentivize decision-making that boosts short-term stock prices at the expense of the company's long-term health and the well-being of its employees and customers.

Erosion of Economic Equality

The mechanisms of Wall Street disproportionately benefit the wealthiest individuals and institutional investors, contributing to widening economic inequality. The wealth generated by rising stock markets and financial sector profits tends to accumulate among those already at the top of the economic ladder, while the risks and negative consequences, such as job losses from corporate restructuring or bailouts during financial crises are socialized among the general public.

Influence on Political Systems

Wall Street's significant financial resources afford it considerable influence over political systems and regulatory frameworks. This influence is often wielded to lobby for deregulation, favorable tax policies, and other legislative changes that benefit the financial sector but may undermine public interests and financial stability. The revolving door between Wall Street and government positions further entrenches the interests of the financial elite within the political and regulatory apparatus, potentially leading to policies that favor the wealthy at the expense of broader societal welfare.

In essence, Wall Street's current operations have caused a range of negative outcomes. These include fostering an environment of short-termism, distorting corporate priorities away from sustainable growth, exacerbating economic inequality, and exerting undue influence on political systems. Addressing these issues requires a concerted effort to realign the incentives and practices of Wall Street with the long-term interests of the economy and society at large.

Problem 8: Bureaucratic insurance

The intertwining of large insurance companies with government regulations exemplifies a concerning trend where corporate interests override public welfare. In a corporatist society, similar to issues seen in non-competitive communist systems, the lack of incentive for quality service becomes stark. This is because insurance companies are guaranteed income through legislations mandating insurance in various sectors, such as car liability and home insurance. The excessive bureaucracy within these corporations not only leads to inefficiencies but also wastes substantial resources that could otherwise benefit society. This relationship between corporations and government regulation fosters an environment where the primary focus shifts from serving the public to maximizing corporate profits, often at the expense of consumer interests and economic efficiency.

Problem 9: Banks

Banks have always played a critical role in the economy. They're the gatekeepers of financial resources, facilitating everything from personal savings to massive corporate investments. There was a day when banks were a necessary. They were once the only secure means of storing money. But modern technology has made their main purpose obsolete. Not only that but banks are inherently corporatist and can be deeply problematic for the health of an economy.

One major issue is that banks have the ability to create money out of thin air through a process called fractional reserve banking. This means they only keep a small fraction of deposits on hand, lending out the rest. On paper, this sounds efficient—it allows more money to circulate in the economy. However, this also means banks are lending money that doesn't actually exist until it's repaid, which can create a house of cards situation. If too many loans go bad, or if there's a sudden demand for withdrawals, the whole system can collapse, leading to financial crises like the ones we saw in 2008 or 1929. These are commonly considered capitalism's biggest failures but they were caused by a corporatist system.

Banks also have a history of exploiting consumers. From charging exorbitant fees to pushing predatory loans, banks often operate with profit as their sole motive, sometimes at the expense of their customers' financial well-being. This behavior deepens economic inequality by trapping the most vulnerable in cycles of debt, while those at the top benefit from the system.

But perhaps the most insidious issue with banks is their influence over government policy. The financial sector spends millions lobbying lawmakers to ensure regulations are favorable to them, often at the expense of the public. This influence can lead to deregulation, which reduces oversight and allows banks to engage in riskier behavior with little fear of consequences.

Banks operate in a way that is strikingly similar to a Ponzi scheme. In a typical Ponzi scheme, money from new investors is used to pay returns to earlier investors, creating the illusion of a profitable business. Banks do something eerily similar with fractional reserve banking. They take deposits from customers and then lend out most of that money, counting on the fact that not everyone will demand their deposits back at the same time. If too many people do, the whole system collapses, much like a Ponzi scheme. What's even more alarming is that while Ponzi schemes are illegal for anyone else to run, banks are not only allowed but are integral to the economy under this very model, propped up by government regulations and protections. Banks take what would normally be considered illegal practices and then are incentivized by bailouts to play riskier and riskier games.

Banks are a blight on the economy, distorting financial stability and perpetuating inequality. Their practices, from creating money out of thin air to influencing government policies in their favor, harm the very foundations of a healthy economic system. Instead of facilitating productive investment, banks often prioritize their profits, leading to cycles of booms and busts that destabilize economies. To build a more equitable and sustainable economy, the power of banks needs to be drastically curtailed, if not entirely removed, allowing for a financial system that genuinely serves the people and promotes long-term growth.

Problem 10: Shrinking Middle Class

The dissonance between GDP growth and the cost of living to income ratio in the United States is stark and telling of a deeper economic malaise. For instance, in the third quarter of 2023, the U.S. economy expanded by an annualized rate of 4.9%, a significant uptick from the 2.1% growth observed in the second quarter of the same year. This figure represents a robust phase of economic expansion, suggesting a healthy, growing economy on the surface. However, this GDP growth does not seem to translate into an improved standard of living for the average American, largely due to the cost of living increases outpacing income growth. To illustrate, while the economy saw considerable growth rates in 2023, real wages—what people can actually buy with their incomes—have remained stagnant when adjusted for inflation over the past several decades. This stagnation occurs despite the productivity and economic output (as measured by GDP) increasing, indicating that the wealth generated by this economic growth is not being evenly distributed across the population.

From 2010 to 2022, home prices in the U.S. increased by 74%, outpacing wage growth, which stood at 54% for the same period. This data reflects a widening gap between living costs and income, emphasizing the affordability crisis many Americans face. During this period, the GDP growth rate varied annually, but the contrast with the cost of living to income ratio growth illustrates the disconnect between overall economic growth and individual economic well-being.

Further, the cost of essential services has skyrocketed. Housing, healthcare, and education costs have seen dramatic increases. For example, the cost of higher education and healthcare has more than doubled in the past few decades, far outpacing the average wage growth. This mismatch between income growth and the cost of living has squeezed the middle class, contributing to its decline. The shrinking middle class is more than an economic statistic; it represents a shift in the economic stability and potential for upward mobility for a significant portion of the population.

The consequence of these dynamics is a growing economic divide, where the benefits of GDP growth are increasingly concentrated among the wealthiest individuals and corporations, leaving the middle class to face the challenges of rising costs without corresponding increases in income. Cost of living to wage ratio has never been worse and yet corporate profits have never been higher.

Sources:

1. Trading Economics. (2023, December 21). United States GDP growth rate. Trading Economics. Retrieved September 3, 2024, from https://tradingeconomics.com/united-states/gdp-growth

2. U.S. Bureau of Economic Analysis. (n.d.). Gross domestic product (GDP). U.S. Department of Commerce. Retrieved September 3, 2024, from https://www.bea.gov/data/gdp/gross-domestic-product

3. USAFacts. (2023, August 30). Housing costs vs. wages. USAFacts. Retrieved September 3, 2024, from https://usafacts.org/data-projects/housing-vs-wages

Problem 11: Merger of Corporation And Government

Lobbying's similarity to bribery becomes most obvious when money overpowers the democratic spirit, forcing the lawmaking process to favor the rich and powerful. This shift is not just a theory but is backed by real examples where lobbying has led to laws and rules that seem to prioritize corporate interests over the public good. The Apple Inc. antitrust battles are a clear example of this issue, showing the serious challenge it presents to governance.

Case Study: Apple and the E-Book Price Fixing Scandal

In April 2012, the United States Department of Justice (DoJ) filed an antitrust lawsuit against Apple Inc. and five major book publishers. The lawsuit claimed that Apple and the publishers worked together to raise, fix, and stabilize retail prices for e-books, breaking Section 1 of the Sherman Antitrust Act. The government's case (United States v. Apple Inc., 12 Civ. 2826 (DLC), 2013) relied on evidence showing that Apple's entry into the e-book market was based on deals that made sure e-book prices across the industry would rise, limiting Amazon's discount pricing model.

The Role of Lobbying

While the case mainly focused on antitrust laws and consumer rights, it also highlighted the heavy lobbying efforts by tech giants like Apple to influence regulatory rules and legislative agendas. For example, Apple's lobbying spending reports, filed with the United States Senate Office of Public Records, show a steady increase in lobbying expenses over the years, reaching a peak during times of significant regulatory attention.

The Impact on Legislation

These lobbying efforts have often led to legislative results that make people question the fairness of the lawmaking process. For instance, the proposed laws around digital marketplaces and antitrust, like the American Innovation and Choice Online Act, have faced intense lobbying from major tech companies, including Apple. Critics say that the detailed positions and changes suggested by these lobbying groups can weaken the effectiveness of laws meant to control monopolistic behavior.

The Problematic Connection

This connection between lobbying and legislative influence becomes especially concerning when it seems to give large companies a veto over rules meant to protect the public. The problem lies in the secretive nature of lobbying, where it's hard to directly link lobbying efforts to legislative outcomes, yet the indirect evidence and patterns of influence are clear.

The Apple case and the broader actions of tech industry lobbying point to a deeper issue where the mix of money, power, and politics can weaken democratic values. This situation calls for a careful review of how lobbying, as it currently operates, might harm the integrity of government decision-making. It highlights the urgent need for major lobbying reform, including stricter disclosure rules, limits on lobbying spending, and closing the "revolving door" between public office and the lobbying industry.

Sources:

1. United States v. Apple Inc., 12 Civ. 2826 (DLC), 2013

2. Lobbying Expenditure Reports

3. United States Senate Office of Public Records

Wall street journal

New york times

Problem 12: Waisted Taxes

Let's take a closer look at what the average American pays in taxes. By the end of 2023, the average salary in the U.S. was around $59,384 per year. On that income, the IRS taxes you at 22% if you're single and earning above $47,150 a year. That's about $13,064.48 in income taxes alone. But that's not where it ends.

Now, let's look at housing. The average home price in the U.S. is around $417,700. Depending on where you live, the property tax rate will vary, but across the country, it averages at 1.003% of the home's value. So, if you own an average home, you're paying around $4,189.53 a year just in property taxes. This already brings the total percentage of income going to taxes to about 29.05% of your salary.

And then, you have sales taxes. Every time you buy groceries, clothes, or everyday essentials, you're paying an average combined sales tax of 6.58% on top of it all. When we add that to our earlier number, we get a 35.63% tax burden. That's more than a third of your annual income gone to taxes before you even start thinking about health insurance, retirement savings, or childcare.

Now, if you listen to a lot of mainstream voices, they'll tell you that higher taxes are a "socialist" thing. They point to countries like Sweden and say their system is oppressive and drains hard-working citizens of their paychecks. But let's compare, shall we?

In Sweden, a socialist-leaning country, individuals pay 0% tax on their first SEK 537,200 (about $48,836 in U.S. dollars). Only income above that amount gets taxed at a rate of 20%. So, if you're making an average U.S. income of $59,384, you'd be paying less in income taxes in Sweden than you would in the United States.

Yet, Sweden's government provides universal healthcare, free higher education, generous parental leave, and robust social safety nets. That's a long list of benefits for less tax than what the average American is paying.

Where Does All the Money Go?

Here's where it gets frustrating: despite paying more in taxes, the average American doesn't enjoy the same benefits as citizens in countries like Sweden. Instead of funding universal healthcare or making education more accessible, much of the U.S. tax revenue disappears into a bureaucratic maze.

For example, the U.S. federal government spends billions annually on bloated defense contracts, which are frequently criticized for their inefficiency and waste. In 2023, the U.S. Department of Defense had a budget of over $800 billion, with much of that going to private contractors, some of which are notorious for overcharging the government.

Additionally, according to the U.S. Government Accountability Office (GAO), federal agencies waste significant amounts of money through improper payments, mismanagement, and inefficient programs. In 2020, the GAO estimated that the government made $175 billion in improper payments—money that should never have been spent. A large defense budget isn't the problem, a careless defense budget is.

So, while Americans are left struggling with expensive healthcare, student debt, and the rising cost of living, their tax dollars aren't being spent in ways that meaningfully improve their lives. Socialism is not the answer, but Americans get taxed a socialist rate and charged a corporatist price.

Sources:

1. IRS Tax Brackets: Internal Revenue Service. (2023). Tax Brackets. [IRS.gov](https://www.irs.gov)

2. Average U.S. Salary: U.S. Bureau of Labor Statistics. (2023). Occupational Employment and Wages, Fourth Quarter. [BLS.gov](https://www.bls.gov)

3. Average Home Price: Federal Reserve Bank of St. Louis. (2023). Median Sales Price of Houses Sold for the United States. [FRED](https://fred.stlouisfed.org/series/MSPUS)

4. Property Taxes: Tax Foundation. (2023). Property Taxes in the United States. [TaxFoundation.org](https://taxfoundation.org)

5. Improper Payments: U.S. Government Accountability Office. (2020). Improper Payments. [GAO.gov](https://www.gao.gov)

Problem 13: The Oligopoly

Oligopoly- a state of limited competition, in which a market is shared by a small number of producers or sellers.

An oligopoly, a market structure dominated by a few entities, inherently risks stifling competition, innovation, and fairness. The alarming ascendancy of oligopolistic dynamics in the global economy casts long shadows over the principles of free market and equitable growth opportunities. This trend towards consolidation of power and wealth among the few not only threatens the democratic fabric of economic participation but also perpetuates a cycle of dependency and vulnerability for the many.

Within the heart of this oligopoly lies BlackRock, an entity whose reach and influence controls almost every sector of the global economy. As the world's largest asset manager, BlackRock's investment decisions echo across the financial markets, influencing the fate of corporations, governments, and by extension, everyday lives. The firm's significant stakes in industries ranging from technology to healthcare illustrate not merely an investment strategy but a blueprint for unparalleled influence over the economic and social spheres.

BlackRock, Vanguard, and State Street, often referred to as the "Big Three" asset management firms, control an unparalleled amount of global wealth and influence. With over $20 trillion in combined assets under management, their reach extends across nearly every major sector of the global economy. These firms hold significant sway over a wide range of industries, from technology and media to energy and pharmaceuticals. Despite their seemingly separate operations, BlackRock and Vanguard are intertwined, with BlackRock owning part of State Street, and Vanguard being a major shareholder in BlackRock. This complex web of ownership highlights the extent of their influence. Below is a detailed breakdown of their control over key industries.

Financial Markets

BlackRock is widely recognized as a dominant force in global financial markets, particularly through its advanced trading algorithm, Aladdin (Asset, Liability, Debt, and Derivative Investment Network). Aladdin, which controls more than $21.6 trillion in assets, is a trading system that executes 250,000 trades per day. It processes vast amounts of data across all asset classes and industries, using machine learning to optimize trades. Aladdin is used by major banks, pension funds, and the Federal Reserve, meaning BlackRock indirectly influences nearly all major financial decisions in the U.S. financial system.

Its power extends to ETFs, where BlackRock controls over half of all Exchange-Traded Funds, while also holding significant sway in the bond market (17%) and stock market (10%). These firms are not just investors; they shape the market itself, making them vital to the functioning of global economies.

Tech Industry

BlackRock, Vanguard, and State Street hold considerable stakes in the technology sector, arguably the most important industry in today's global economy. They are the top shareholders in tech giants such as Alphabet (Google's parent company), Apple, Microsoft, Facebook, IBM, and AT&T. Their collective ownership allows them to exert considerable influence over the strategic direction of these companies, especially in areas of innovation, data privacy, and technology ethics.

For instance, Vanguard and BlackRock together own large portions of Microsoft and Apple, two of the largest companies in the world by market capitalization. In an era where technology dictates much of modern life, their power within this sector cannot be overstated. By having significant stakes in so many technology companies, they are well-positioned to guide the future of AI, cloud computing, and even cybersecurity.

Pharmaceutical and Health Industry

In the pharmaceutical industry, Vanguard is the largest shareholder in some of the world's biggest healthcare companies, holding 8.89% of Johnson & Johnson, 8.95% of Merck & Co., 8.97% of AbbVie, and 10% of CVS Health. BlackRock typically follows closely behind as the second-largest shareholder in these companies.

This extensive ownership allows both firms to influence critical decisions related to drug pricing, healthcare policies, and research and development. The sheer scale of their investments in pharmaceuticals gives them a powerful voice in the future of global healthcare, particularly in areas like vaccine development, biotechnology, and medical research.

Food Industry

BlackRock, Vanguard, and State Street are major shareholders in some of the largest food and beverage companies in the world. For example, BlackRock holds 7.2% of Tyson Foods, Vanguard holds 9.29% of PepsiCo's shares, making it the company's largest shareholder, while BlackRock holds 7.84%. In Coca-Cola, the two firms hold a combined 15.7%, with Vanguard at 8.51% and BlackRock at 7.19%. The dominance of these firms extends to other food giants such as Unilever, Mondelez, Nestlé, General Mills, Hershey, and Kraft Heinz.

This concentrated ownership gives BlackRock and Vanguard significant influence over the direction of these companies, including their business strategies, environmental policies, and corporate governance. Given the global scale of the food industry, this ownership translates into control over much of what consumers see on grocery store shelves worldwide.

Energy Industry

In the energy sector, BlackRock and Vanguard's influence is equally substantial. BlackRock alone has invested $170 billion in U.S. public energy companies, with $85 billion dedicated to coal companies as of 2021. Together, BlackRock, Vanguard, and State Street control significant portions of oil giants such as ExxonMobil, Chevron, ConocoPhillips, and Occidental Petroleum.

These firms also hold $46 billion in debt and equity in companies that operate within the Amazon rainforest, a region critical to global environmental health. Their collective investments in fossil fuels amount to nearly $260 billion worldwide, placing them at the heart of debates surrounding climate change and environmental responsibility. Despite increasing pressures for sustainable investing, their considerable holdings in coal, oil, and gas reveal a deep connection to the traditional energy sector.

Media Industry

Perhaps one of the most concerning aspects of BlackRock and Vanguard's dominance is their role in the media industry. The two firms are the top shareholders in four of the six major companies that control over 90% of the U.S. media landscape: Time Warner, Comcast, Disney, and News Corp. Together, BlackRock and Vanguard own 18% of Fox, 16% of CBS, 13% of Comcast (which owns NBC, MSNBC, CNBC, and Sky Media Group), 12% of CNN, and 12% of Disney.

This level of ownership raises significant questions about the role of these firms in shaping public discourse and information flow. In addition to their U.S. holdings, they own stakes in international media outlets such as VTM and Mediahuis in Europe. BlackRock also owns Bertelsmann, a major German conglomerate that controls RTL, which operates 45 television stations and 32 radio stations across 11 countries. Bertelsmann is also a co-owner of Penguin Random House, the largest book publisher in the world.

Travel Industry

BlackRock and Vanguard's influence extends to the travel industry as well. The two firms together own 21% of Expedia Group, 15% of Booking Holdings, 27% of American Express,

13% of Boeing, 10% of Airbnb, and 16% of TripAdvisor. Their control over these companies allows them to shape the global travel market, affecting everything from airline operations to hotel bookings and credit services related to travel.

Government and Political Influence

Their influence isn't confined to the private sector. As of 2021, at least three executives from BlackRock hold high-level positions in the Biden administration, including Brian Deese as the Head of the National Economic Council and Adewale Adeyemo as the Deputy Treasury Secretary. These appointments blur the line between the private financial sector and public policy, raising concerns about potential conflicts of interest.

BlackRock's influence over central banks is also noteworthy. The firm not only lends money to central banks but also advises them and develops the software they use. This deep integration with the financial system makes BlackRock a critical player in shaping both monetary policy and financial regulation globally.

Corporate Takeovers and Acquisitions

BlackRock and Vanguard have also expanded their reach through acquisitions. BlackRock has acquired 21 companies to date, including the purchase of Aperio for $1 billion in 2020 and eFront for $1.3 billion in 2019. Perhaps most notably, BlackRock acquired Barclays Global Investors in 2009, including its iShares ETF business, solidifying its dominance in the ETF market. These acquisitions have only increased their market influence, allowing them to shape the future of asset management on a global scale.

Overall Market Ownership

BlackRock, Vanguard, and State Street—often referred to as the "Big Three"—have amassed an unprecedented level of power through their vast ownership of U.S. publicly traded companies. They are the largest shareholders in at least 40% of all publicly listed firms and hold an even greater share in the S&P 500, where their collective ownership often reaches 20-25% of individual companies. This level of control gives them extraordinary influence over corporate governance, as their voting power in shareholder meetings can sway key decisions that affect everything from executive pay to company policies. Their sheer dominance in the passive index fund market, where they manage over 80-90% of assets, cements their role as gatekeepers of corporate America.

What makes this concentration of ownership even more powerful is that their influence often extends beyond shareholder votes. With such significant stakes, these asset managers hold substantial sway over corporate leaders, who regularly engage with them behind closed doors. Even though the Big Three typically support management in public votes, their private interactions can shape company strategies in ways that are invisible to the public. This quiet yet far-reaching control has sparked concerns about the potential consequences for market competition, financial stability, and the concentration of economic power in a few hands.

Conclusion

The combined influence of BlackRock, Vanguard, and State Street forms a financial and political pyramid, where smaller investors are owned by larger ones, all ultimately controlled by the same few powerful entities. These firms' extensive holdings and interlocking ownership structures give them first-mover advantages in nearly every major industry, from technology and media to healthcare and energy. As a result, BlackRock and Vanguard are not just financial giants; they are central players in the global economy, with the ability to shape markets, influence policy, and direct the future of some of the most critical sectors in the world.

Sources:

1. Chitnis, O. (n.d.). Giant conglomerates control the world. LinkedIn. Retrieved March 18, 2024, from https://www.linkedin.com/pulse/giant-conglomerates-control-world-omkar-chitnis

2. Bloomberg. (n.d.). Markets. Bloomberg. Retrieved March 18, 2024, from http://bloomberg.com/Markets

3. Yahoo Finance. (n.d.). Yahoo Finance. Retrieved March 18, 2024, from https://finance.yahoo.com/

4. World Bank. (n.d.). World Bank. Retrieved March 18, 2024, from https://www.worldbank.org/

5. Koyfin. (n.d.). Koyfin. Retrieved March 18, 2024, from https://www.koyfin.com/

6. Fintel. (n.d.). BlackRock Inc. ownership in TSN / Tyson Foods, Inc.. Fintel. Retrieved March 18, 2024, from https://fintel.io/tsn/blackrock

7. Reuters. (2021, January 26). Introducing a new Reuters.com. Reuters. Retrieved March 18, 2024, from https://www.reuters.com/

8. IESE Insight article:

Azar, José, and Jara-Bertin, Mauricio. "Common Shareholders in Rival Companies: Are They a Threat?" IESE Insight. [https://www.iese.edu](https://www.iese.edu/insight/articles/common-shareholders-rival-companies-threat/).

9. Harvard Law School Forum on Corporate Governance:
Bebchuk, Lucian A., and Hirst, Scott. "Index Funds and the Future of Corporate Governance: Theory, Evidence, and Policy." Harvard Law School Forum on Corporate Governance, April 13, 2022. [https://corpgov.law.harvard.edu](https://corpgov.law.harvard.edu/2022/04/13/__trashed/).

10. Cambridge Journal of Business and Politics article:
Fichtner, Jan, Heemskerk, Eelke M., and Garcia-Bernardo, Javier. "The Hidden Power of the Big Three? Passive Index Funds, Re-concentration of Corporate Ownership, and New Financial Risk." Business and Politics, vol. 19, no. 2, 2017, pp. 298–326. [https://www.cambridge.org](https://www.cambridge.org/core/journals/business-and-politics/article/hidden-power-of-the-big-three-passive-index-funds-reconcentration-of-corporate-ownership-and-new-financial-risk/30AD689509AAD62F5B677E916C28C4B6).

Final Problem: The Great Depression

If none of the above problems were enough to convince you maybe this will. It's currently harder financially to live than in the Great Depression. Don't believe me?

Average Income
1930: $4,887
Adjusted for Inflation (2024): ~$88,000
2024: $56,000

2. Average Cost of Living
1930: ~$4,000 annually
Adjusted for Inflation (2024): ~$69,600
2024: ~$60,575

3. Average Home Price
1930: $3,900
Adjusted for Inflation (2024): ~$65,000
2024: ~$436,000

4. Average Tuition Cost (Public Four-Year College)
1930: ~$400 annually
Adjusted for Inflation (2024): ~$6,700
2024: ~$11,360

5. Average Car Cost
1930: $600
Adjusted for Inflation (2024): ~$10,000

2024: ~$48,000

6. Average Grocery Cost (Annual for a Family)
1930: ~$300
Adjusted for Inflation (2024): ~$5,000
2024: ~$4,750

In almost all of these categories it is harder to live than in the middle of the Great Depression. Yet people say there's no problem. Politicians claim we are at the height of the US economy. There is no doubting the fact that there is a problem. The question is, how do we fix it?

Sources:

- Business Anthropology Network, 2023. https://www.businessanthropology.net
- Consumer Affairs, 2024. https://www.consumeraffairs.com
- Inflation Data, 2024. https://inflationdata.com
- Visual Capitalist, 2024. https://www.visualcapitalist.com
- Isabel Brown. (2023, September 7). Are Americans today making less than at the height of the Great Depression? Politifact. https://www.politifact.com/factchecks/2023/sep/07/isabel-brown/are-americans-today-making-less-than-at-the-height/
- What was the average wage in 1930? Study.com. https://homework.study.com/explanation/what-was-the-average-wage-in-1930.html:~:text=Answer
- Americans are being gaslit into thinking we're too entitled or expecting too much. Yahoo Finance. https://finance.yahoo.com/news/americans-being-gaslit-thinking-were-132459774.html:~:text=D

3

A Better Way

Savaism: An economic system which incentivizes reinvestment of wealth rather than the hoarding of the elite, built upon the idea that there is enough to go around if the economy would foster wealth reinvestment.

Savaism is an economic philosophy built on the idea that prosperity doesn't have to be a zero-sum game. It challenges the traditional divide between socialism and corporatism by proposing a third path: an economy where wealth is not forcibly redistributed, but instead naturally reinvested. In this system, the role of government isn't to take from the rich and give to the poor; rather, it ensures that the rich cannot exploit the poor in the first place. The key to Savaism lies in a few key remedies. These economic fixes will build upon the current economic model and will help to build an environment where wealth flows back into society, driving growth, innovation, and opportunity for all, without the need for heavy-handed intervention.

Summary

Savaism presents a revolutionary economic and governance model designed to recalibrate the foundational principles of society towards cooperation, equity, and sustainable growth. At its core, Savaism seeks to dismantle the structures that perpetuate corporate greed, economic inequality, and the undue influence of wealth in politics, replacing them with mechanisms that foster communal prosperity and direct democratic participation.

Economic Principles:

- Elimination of Traditional Corporate and Financial Structures: Savaism proposes the abolition of IPOs, dividends, and the traditional banking systems which take advantage of the middle class. As well as abolishing these unfair systems savaism will aim to prohibit corporations from owning residential real estate. This approach aims to curb artificial inflation and

prevent the concentration of wealth, creating a more level playing field for all members of society.
- Decentralized, GDP-Backed Currency: The introduction of a blockchain-protected, GDP-backed decentralized currency limits government interference in monetary policy and ensures a stable, equitable financial system. The currency's growth is tied directly to the nation's economic performance, with a controlled inflation rate to preserve purchasing power.
- Restructuring Corporate Ownership: Transitioning corporations into A-Corps and limiting income disparities (with the highest incomes capped at 100 times the median income) aims to distribute wealth more evenly and align business incentives with societal well-being.
- Simplification of Taxation: By implementing a tax system based on a flat sales tax, Savaism simplifies the tax system, enhancing transparency and efficiency while eliminating the need for complex taxation mechanisms and bureaucracies like the IRS.
- Enforcement of Anti-Trust Laws: Recognizing the importance of competition for innovation and growth, Savaism emphasizes the need for effective enforcement of anti-trust laws to prevent monopolies and ensure a diverse, dynamic market environment.

Social and Cultural Principles:

- Promotion of Cooperation: By fundamentally restructuring economic incentives and governance mechanisms, Savaism fosters a societal ethos that values cooperation, community well-being, and sustainable development over individual gain.

Savaism represents a bold reimagining of societal organization, aiming to create an environment where economic power is genuinely democratized, and the prosperity generated is shared equitably among all citizens. This vision for a more cooperative, just, and sustainable society challenges existing paradigms, offering a blueprint for a future defined by collective success and harmony.

The 11 principles of Savaism:

1. Fair Tax Policies: A simplified tax system based on a flat sales tax, removing multiple forms of taxation to ensure transparency and fairness.

2. Non-Profit Regulation of Essential Services: Essential services like healthcare, insurance, and pharmaceuticals must operate as non-profits, ensuring affordability and accessibility.

3. Reform of Anti-Trust Laws: Strengthening anti-trust laws to prevent monopolies and promote competition, fostering innovation and diversity in the market.

4. Criminalization of Campaign Donations: Strict regulations to sever the connection between money and politics, ensuring a government that truly represents the people.

5. Abolition of the Stock Market: Preventing speculative stock ownership to promote long-term economic stability and prevent financial exploitation.

6. Abolition of the Banking System: Eliminating the borrow culture in the US by removing these highly volatile immoral institutions.

7. Decentralization of Currency: Moving to decentralized currency models to reduce government control over monetary policy, encouraging financial freedom.

8. Introduction of a GDP-Backed Stable Coin: A stable coin linked to the nation's GDP, offering a secure, inflation-controlled financial tool.

9. Prohibition on Corporate Ownership of Residential Property: Corporations would be banned from owning residential properties to preserve affordability and community ownership.

10. Restructuring Government Financial Oversight: Abolishing institutions like the IRS and Federal Reserve, replacing them with streamlined government financial oversight for efficiency.

11. Corporate Reorganization into A-Corp: Transitioning corporations into a new fair form of company called A-Corps which have correlated Income Ratios. Any owners' draws, dividends, or money payouts from A-Corps would be classified as legal income. However, these incomes would be capped at 100 times the median income, using Outlier Detection and Exclusion methods and a trimmed mean to prevent excessive pay at the top.

Principle 1: Fairer Tax Policies

Savaism advocates for a complete overhaul of the existing tax system, proposing the adoption of fair tax policies characterized by a simplified, equitable approach. The cornerstone of this reform is the introduction of a flat sales tax, which replaces the deceptive layers of current taxes—such as income tax, capital gains tax, property tax, and others—with a single, transparent tax on consumption. This model is designed to streamline the tax collection process, making it more understandable for citizens and easier to administer for the government.

Key Features and Implications:

- Simplicity and Transparency: The flat sales tax simplifies the tax code, making it easier for individuals and businesses to comply with their tax obligations. This transparency fosters a greater understanding of taxation among the populace, reducing confusion and the burden of compliance.

- Equitable Tax Burden: By shifting to a consumption-based tax model, the tax burden is distributed more evenly across different income groups. While care must be taken to ensure essential goods and services remain accessible to lower-income individuals, this model aims to create a fairer taxation system where the amount of tax paid is directly related to consumption levels.

- Efficiency in Tax Collection: The consolidation of multiple taxes into a single flat sales tax enhances the efficiency of tax collection, potentially reducing administrative costs and the opportunities for tax evasion. This efficiency can lead to a more effective allocation of resources within the government, potentially funding public services and infrastructure more robustly.

- Economic Impact: By eliminating taxes on income and investment, the fair tax policies could encourage savings and investment, contributing to economic growth. However, the impact on consumer spending must be carefully monitored to ensure the tax does not disproportionately discourage consumption.

This book is not actually the first proposal of an idea like this. A bill by the name of The Fair Tax Act, introduced as far back as 1999, aimed to replace the complex tax system with a straightforward national sales tax, eliminating income, payroll, and other taxes. Its goal was to simplify taxation and promote fairness by shifting the burden from income to consumption. Despite these potential benefits, the proposal has been continually blocked by our divided government. This political deadlock is a frustrating reflection of the duality in our legislative system, where bold ideas are often stifled, not due to their merit but because of partisan gridlock. The failure to pass the Fair Tax Act represents a missed opportunity for transformative tax reform, leaving us stuck with an outdated and inefficient system that burdens individuals and businesses alike.

Overall, the implementation of fair tax policies under Savaism represents a radical departure from traditional tax systems, aiming to foster a more equitable, transparent, and efficient fiscal environment. This reform is intended to support the broader objectives of Savaism, including promoting economic equality and simplifying government bureaucracy, thereby aligning the tax structure with the principles of fairness and cooperation that underpin the ideology.

Sources:

- Cole, A. (2023, May 11). The FairTax? - The Deduction. Tax Foundation. Retrieved from https://taxfoundation.org/fair-tax-national-sales-tax/

- Hodge, S. (2023, July 24). Tax Reform: Flat Tax or FairTax? Tax Foundation. Retrieved from https://taxfoundation.org/fair-tax-plan-national-sales-tax/

- Morgan, K. (2023). What Is the FairTax Act? Pros & Cons. Money Crashers. Retrieved from https://www.moneycrashers.com/fair-tax-act/

- Tax Policy Center. (2023). What is the Fair Tax? Retrieved from https://www.taxpolicycenter.org/briefing-book/what-fair-tax

Principal 2: Non-Profit Requirements on Essential Services

Under Savaism, a transformative approach is adopted in sectors deemed critical for public welfare—such as healthcare, insurance, education, and pharmaceuticals—are mandated to operate under non-profit models. This pivotal reform aims to prioritize access, affordability, and quality in essential services, ensuring that these sectors serve the public interest above profit motives.

Key Features and Implications:

- Public Interest Over Profit: By transitioning to non-profit models, essential service providers are reoriented towards serving the public good. This model inherently reduces the incentive to inflate prices for the sake of profit, potentially leading to more affordable and accessible services for all citizens.

- Enhanced Quality of Service: Without the pressure to generate profit for shareholders, organizations can focus on improving the quality of service and investing in innovation that directly benefits consumers and patients. This could lead to significant advancements in public health and welfare.

- Regulatory Oversight: The successful implementation of this model requires robust regulatory frameworks to ensure these organizations truly prioritize public welfare. This includes oversight of operations, pricing, and the reinvestment of any surpluses back into service improvements or expansion.

- Economic and Social Impact: Transitioning to a non-profit model in these critical sectors may have profound implications for the economy and society. It could lead to a more equitable distribution of resources and mitigate some of the adverse effects of income inequality. Furthermore, by ensuring that essential services are not subject to market volatility and profit-driven compromises, societal well-being can be significantly enhanced.

Savaism are focuses on creating non-profit healthcare to offer affordable healthcare without burdening taxpayers or inflating the economy. In the current system, a significant portion of the profits in healthcare goes to corporate executives and shareholders. For example, the U.S. healthcare industry generated a projected $654 billion in profits in 2021, which is expected to rise to $790 billion by 2026. Much of this profit ends up in the hands of healthcare executives, major companies like UnitedHealth Group and CVS Health, and shareholders.

This setup drives costs higher because the focus is on maximizing returns for investors rather than improving patient care. In fact, many insurers and hospitals spend a disproportionate amount of their revenue, sometimes as high as 85% on administrative costs, a large portion of which is profit payouts to executives and investors.

The vision with Savaism is to remove the profit motive from these essential services. By transforming healthcare, education, insurance, and similar services into non-profits, we ensure that funds go directly to improving services, reducing costs for patients, and ensuring accessibility, rather than lining the pockets of the elite. This approach avoids the need for the government to raise taxes or borrow money just to cover inflated healthcare costs driven by private sector profits.

Every solution to these sectors becoming too expensive has involved the government covering the costs, but no one stopped to question why they were high in the first place. They say there's no such thing as a free lunch. When the government covers these costs, it ultimately comes back to the public, all so a few billionaires can make more money. Instead of having the government pay, the focus should be on ensuring these costs never get that high in the first place by shifting to a nonprofit business model.

Challenges and Considerations:

You may read this and become concerned. Won't this lower the incentive to scale these essential services? Couldn't this result in lowering accessibility to said services? While this concern is valid, it is not accurate. I know this because some of the most successful healthcare companies in the world are already nonprofit or not-for-profit. For example, Kaiser Permanente, the largest nonprofit healthcare system in the U.S., operates with over $100 billion in revenue, ranking it higher than many for-profit healthcare companies. Similarly, CommonSpirit Health and Ascension, two other major nonprofit systems, consistently place among the top 20 largest healthcare organizations nationwide, proving that nonprofit models can scale just as efficiently as their for-profit counterparts. These organizations deliver high-quality care while reinvesting profits back into services, technology, and patient outcomes rather than shareholders. By focusing on community health over profit margins, they set the standard for both financial success and service accountability.

If these companies are already nonprofit then why are they still expensive? While nonprofit healthcare systems like Kaiser Permanente and CommonSpirit Health operate efficiently and reinvest in patient care, they are still subject to the same costly healthcare industry standards. Medical equipment, pharmaceuticals, and insurance premiums remain incredibly expensive, bottlenecking their ability to lower patient costs. For instance, pharmaceutical prices in the U.S. are often twice as high as in other countries thanks to corporatism, and the cost of medical technologies continues to rise. These nonprofit systems face the same financial burdens as their for-profit counterparts, meaning they must still charge competitive rates to cover these costs. The nonprofit model can only achieve its full potential if all players—manufacturers, insurers, and policymakers—commit to fair pricing standards across the board. Otherwise, these essential services will remain financially strained despite their nonprofit status.

The implementation of non-profit regulation in essential services represents a core principle of Savaism, aimed at redefining the relationship between the economy and the welfare of the citizenry. This approach underscores the belief that access to healthcare, insurance, and pharmaceuticals is a fundamental right, not a privilege to be commodified. By enshrining these sectors as non-profit, Savaism seeks to create a society where essential services are universally accessible, and their provision is aligned with the needs and health of the community rather than the dictates of the market.

Sources:

1. Business Chief North America. (2023, June 26). US healthcare in 2023: Profit projections and industry outlook. Business Chief. https://www.businesschief.com

2. Mark Farrah Associates. (2023). 2023 health insurance segment profitability. Mark Farrah Associates. https://www.markfarrah.com

3. American Hospital Association (AHA). (2023). 2023 costs of caring. American Hospital Association. https://www.aha.org

4. Becker's Hospital Review. (2024, February 12). Kaiser Permanente posts $4.1B net income in 2023. https://www.beckershospitalreview.com/kaiser-posts-41b-net-income-in-2023

5. Fierce Healthcare. (2023, February 9). Kaiser Permanente exceeds $100B operating revenues in 2023. https://www.fiercehealthcare.com/providers/kaiser-permanente-reports-41b-profit-exceeds-100b-operating-revenues-2023

6. McKinsey & Company. (2021). Administrative expenses in the US healthcare system: Why so high? https://www.mckinsey.com/industries/healthcare-systems-

and-services/our-insights/reducing-administrative-spending-in-us-healthcare

7. Commonwealth Fund. (2021). High U.S. healthcare spending: Where is it all going? https://www.commonwealthfund.org/publications/high-us-healthcare-spending

8. Becker's Hospital Review. (2023, June 7). Fortune 500's top 25 healthcare companies. Becker's Healthcare. https://www.beckershospitalreview.com/rankings-and-ratings/fortune-500-s-top-25-healthcare-companies.html:contentReference{index=2}

9. Becker's Hospital Review. (2023). 100 largest hospitals and health systems in the US. Becker's Healthcare. https://www.beckershospitalreview.com/lists/100-largest-hospitals-and-health-systems-in-the-us-2023.html:contentReference{index=3}

10. The Healthy Muse. (2022). The 19 largest health systems in 2022. The Healthy Muse. https://thehealthymuse.com/the-largest-health-systems-in-america:contentReference{index=4}

Principal 3: Reformation of Strong anti-Trust Laws

Savaism emphasizes the critical need to strengthen and effectively enforce anti-trust laws to ensure a competitive market landscape. This initiative aims to dismantle monopolistic practices and prevent the concentration of market power that stifles innovation, inflates prices, and undermines the principles of equitable economic participation.

Key Features and Implications:

- Strengthening Legal Frameworks: The reform involves revising existing anti-trust legislation to close loopholes that allow for anti-competitive behavior. This may include clearer definitions of monopolistic practices, stricter penalties for violations, and expanded powers for regulatory bodies to investigate and dismantle monopolies and oligopolies.

- Enhanced Enforcement Mechanisms: Beyond legislative reform, Savaism calls for bolstering the resources and authority of regulatory agencies tasked with enforcing anti-trust laws. This ensures that these agencies have the necessary tools to effectively monitor markets, conduct thorough investigations, and enforce compliance with anti-trust regulations.

- Promotion of Market Competition: By actively preventing the concentration of market power, these reforms aim to foster a dynamic and competitive business environment. This is crucial for stimulating innovation, ensuring small and medium-sized enterprises have fair opportunities to grow, and preventing the exploitation of consumers through inflated pricing or reduced choice.

- Balancing Economic Power: The application of anti-trust laws under Savaism is intended to redistribute economic power more evenly across society. By preventing large corporations from dominating markets, it ensures that economic benefits and opportunities are more widely accessible, supporting Savaism's broader goals of cooperation and equity.

Societal Benefits:

The effective enforcement of anti-trust laws is expected to lead to a more equitable distribution of wealth and opportunity, reduced cost of living through more competitive pricing, and a surge in innovation as companies vie to offer superior products and services. Moreover, it aligns with Savaism's ethos of diminishing excessive corporate influence in both the economy and governance, ensuring that the market serves the public interest.

Reforming antitrust laws under Savaism would essentially mean undoing the damage caused by corporate lobbyists over the years. These lobbyists have worked to weaken regulations and carve out loopholes that allow big corporations to consolidate power and stifle competition. By restoring the original intent of antitrust laws, we would be dismantling the monopolistic structures that lobbyists have built, creating a fairer marketplace where innovation and small businesses can thrive. This process reverses years of corporate influence over lawmakers, ensuring that the economy benefits the public, not just the elite.

In essence, the reform of anti-trust laws in Savaism represents a foundational shift towards a more inclusive and fair economic system. It acknowledges the critical role of healthy competition in driving progress and prosperity, while actively working to prevent the economic imbalance and social injustices that can arise from unchecked corporate power.

Principle 4: The Criminalization of Campaign Donations

In the pursuit of a purer form of democracy, Savaism introduces a radical reform by criminalizing certain types of campaign donations. This bold move aims to sever the connections between economic wealth and political power, ensuring that political influence cannot be bought and that the electoral process remains a true reflection of the people's will.

Key Features and Implications:

- Restrictions on Political Financing: This reform entails setting strict legal boundaries around the financing of political campaigns, specifically targeting large donations from corporations and wealthy individuals. By criminalizing these donations, Savaism seeks to prevent undue influence over political candidates and elected officials, fostering a political landscape where ideas and policies are paramount, not financial backing.

- Enhanced Political Equity: By eliminating the financial arms race that characterizes many political campaigns, candidates can compete on a more level playing field. This opens the political arena to a broader array of candidates, including those from less affluent backgrounds, thereby enriching the democratic process with diverse perspectives and priorities.

- Increased Public Trust: Public faith in the democratic process is bolstered when citizens can trust that elected officials are serving the public interest, not repaying the financial backers who helped them get into office. Criminalizing significant campaign donations is a direct approach to rebuilding this trust, emphasizing the value of each vote over the size of each donation.

- Transparency and Accountability: With the criminalization of large campaign donations, political financing becomes more transparent. Candidates and political parties are encouraged—or required—to rely more on small donations from a broad base of supporters, making their financial backing and the influences upon them more transparent to the electorate.

Challenges and Considerations:

While the intention behind this reform is to enhance democracy, its implementation must be carefully designed to ensure it does not inadvertently stifle legitimate political expression or participation. Ensuring that mechanisms are in place for small-scale, grassroots funding is essential to maintain vibrant political engagement and competition.

Conclusion:

Criminalizing significant campaign donations is a cornerstone of Savaism's strategy to reform democracy, aiming to dismantle the pervasive influence of money in politics. This reform seeks not only to ensure that elected representatives genuinely represent the interests of their constituents but also to restore integrity and trust in the political process. By redefining the parameters of political campaigning, Savaism lays the groundwork for a more equitable and representative governance model.

Principle 5: Abolition of the stock market

Abolition of the Stock Market

A fundamental aspect of Savaism's economic reform is the complete abolition of the stock market. The stock market, which often fosters speculative financial practices, has been a key contributor to economic instability and inequality. By dismantling this system, Savaism seeks to build a more stable and equitable economic environment.

Key Features and Implications:

- Eliminating Speculation: Without the stock market, the economy would no longer be driven by speculative investment that prioritizes short-term gains over long-term economic health. Instead, capital would be directed toward productive investments in businesses, infrastructure, and sustainable projects that deliver real value to society.

- Focus on Real Economic Growth: The abolition of the stock market would shift the focus away from trading on fluctuating market prices and toward creating tangible goods and services. Businesses would no longer be beholden to shareholders demanding quick profits, allowing them to invest in long-term growth, innovation, and job creation.

- Reducing Economic Inequality: The stock market has long been a vehicle for concentrating wealth among a small elite, with those who own and trade stocks benefiting disproportionately from economic growth. By eliminating this system, Savaism aims to distribute wealth more equitably, ensuring that economic prosperity is shared across society rather than hoarded by a few.

- Enhancing Financial Stability: The volatile nature of stock markets has led to frequent financial crises, driven by bubbles and crashes that have devastating effects on the economy and people's livelihoods. By abolishing the stock market, Savaism would reduce the risk of these speculative-driven crises, creating a more stable and resilient financial system.

The stock market is really just a modern Ponzi scheme, designed to keep pulling in new money to sustain itself, but it's fundamentally unstable. The numbers don't lie: U.S. stocks are valued at $55 trillion, while there are only $2.35 trillion in actual dollars circulating. What does that mean? It means if everyone decided to cash out at once, the system would collapse because the money simply doesn't exist.

This isn't just about numbers, it's about how the system is rigged. The stock market creates the illusion of wealth, but most of it is speculative—money that doesn't exist until someone else buys in. This constant need for new buyers to prop up the value is exactly how a Ponzi scheme operates. And when the market takes a dive, it's regular people who get wiped out, while the wealthy insiders cash out early.

Even if the government wanted to step in with bailouts, it wouldn't be enough. The U.S. Treasury is already stretched thin with over $23.7 trillion in debt. The truth is, the system can't support itself long-term, and bailouts only mask the problem. This isn't some stable, reliable system—it's a house of cards built on the hope that not everyone tries to cash out at once. And the moment that happens, it all crumbles.

When you really look at the numbers, it's clear: the stock market isn't about real value, it's about keeping the illusion alive as long as possible.

Challenges and Considerations:

Transitioning away from a stock market-driven economy requires significant changes in the way capital invested. Savaism would promote alternative funding models that emphasize long-term investment in productive assets, while also addressing resistance from established financial interests that have benefited from the current system.

Conclusion:

The abolition of the stock market represents a bold and transformative step toward refocusing the economy on sustainable, equitable growth. By eliminating speculative financial practices, Savaism fosters an economic environment that prioritizes the real needs of society and ensures that wealth is distributed more fairly. This reform is central to Savaism's vision of a more stable, just, and prosperous economy for all.

Sources:

Siblis Research. (2024, September 11). US stock market total market value (2024). Siblis Research. https://siblisresearch.com/data/us-stock-market-value/

Board of Governors of the Federal Reserve System (US). (2024, September 26). Currency in circulation [Data set]. FRED, Federal Reserve Bank of St. Louis. https://fred.stlouisfed.org/series/CURRCIR

Center on Budget and Policy Priorities. (2023, March). Policy basics: Where do our federal tax dollars go? https://www.cbpp.org

Principle 6: Abolition of Banks

A fundamental aspect of Savaism's economic reform is the abolition of banks. In modern America, banks have evolved from useful financial institutions into debt-driving machines that fuel price inflation and trap individuals in a cycle of borrowing. What was once a system for safeguarding wealth and providing returns has become an exploitative Ponzi scheme that relies on constant borrowing to survive. By eliminating banks, Savaism aims to break the grip of this debt culture and establish a fairer, more sustainable economy.

Key Features and Implications:

- Eliminating Borrow Culture: In today's economy, loans are essential for everything—from buying a home to paying for education and healthcare. However, this reliance on borrowing has distorted how businesses and industries set prices. Corporations no longer charge what it costs to make a product or provide a service; instead, they charge what people are able to borrow. This artificial price inflation is worsened by banks, which profit from issuing loans with interest, locking consumers into perpetual debt. Savaism seeks to eradicate this debt culture by removing banks from the equation, ensuring that prices reflect real value rather than inflated figures based on borrowing limits.

- Ending the Banking Ponzi Scheme: Banks operate much like a Ponzi scheme, relying on constant new deposits and loans to cover their obligations. They promise returns that they can rarely sustain, and when their system falters, as it did during the 2008 financial crisis, taxpayer-funded bailouts are required to prop them up. These bailouts shift the burden of a failing system onto the public, while the wealthiest benefit. By abolishing banks, Savaism will prevent future economic crises driven by unsustainable financial practices and ensure that wealth is distributed more equitably throughout society.

- Obsolete Financial Services: Technology has rendered much of what banks used to provide—like safe money storage and financial returns—obsolete. Digital platforms and financial technology (FinTech) now allow people to manage and store their wealth more securely and efficiently without the need for middlemen. Additionally, interest rates on savings accounts have plummeted, meaning banks no longer offer substantial returns on deposits. Savaism acknowledges that banks are no longer necessary for wealth management, and their elimination would reduce fees, streamline financial transactions, and give individuals more control over their resources.

- Real Estate and Price Manipulation: The housing market provides a clear example of how banks inflate prices. Home values are not based on real costs but on what buyers can finance through loans. As banks make borrowing easier, housing prices skyrocket, making homeownership unattainable for many. Without banks driving this artificial demand, real estate prices would stabilize, reflecting true market value. By abolishing banks, Savaism would prevent future housing bubbles and ensure that real estate remains affordable for all.

America's Debt Crisis

The U.S. has one of the highest debt-to-income ratios in the world, with the average household carrying over $100,000 in debt. This burden is unsustainable and fuels a cycle of dependency on loans and credit. Banks profit enormously from this setup, but the average American struggles to stay afloat, as more income is funneled into paying off debts rather than being reinvested in communities. This debt-fueled system disproportionately benefits the financial elite while undermining the financial security of the majority.

Challenges and Considerations

Transitioning away from a bank-driven economy will require significant restructuring of financial systems. Community-based financial models, technology-driven platforms, and anti bank regulations. This type of legislation will prove difficult to pass because of the grip these corporations have on the federal government.

Conclusion

The abolition of banks under Savaism represents a radical shift toward a fairer economy. By ending debt culture, eliminating artificial price inflation, and preventing future financial crises, Savaism aims to create a system that works for everyone, not just the financial elite. Banks, which were once useful, have become parasitic institutions that no longer add value to the economy. The future of finance is one of decentralization and community empowerment, not bank-driven exploitation.

Sources:

Debt.org. (2022). Debt in America: Statistics and demographics. https://www.debt.org/

World Economic Forum. (2020). How big is America's public debt? https://www.weforum.org/reports

Principle 7: Decentralization of Currency:

Savaism proposes a groundbreaking shift in monetary policy through the decentralization of currency. This approach aims to democratize financial power by moving away from centralized banking systems and towards a model where currency issuance and management are distributed across a network, leveraging blockchain technology for security and transparency.

Key Features and Implications:

- Reduction of Centralized Control: By decentralizing currency, Savaism seeks to reduce the influence of central banks and governmental institutions on the economy. This model limits the ability of a central authority to manipulate currency supply, interest rates, and inflation, thereby aiming to create a more stable economic environment that is less susceptible to policy-induced volatility.

- Use of Blockchain Technology: The decentralized currency system relies on blockchain technology to ensure the integrity, security, and transparency of transactions. Blockchain's decentralized nature makes it resistant to fraud and corruption, offering a robust framework for managing the currency without centralized oversight.

- Empowerment of Individuals and Communities: Decentralizing currency aligns with Savaism's ethos of empowering individuals and communities by giving them greater control over their financial transactions and the economic resources within their localities. This approach encourages financial inclusion and grassroots economic development.

- Innovation in Financial Services: The decentralization of currency paves the way for innovative financial services and products that can operate outside traditional banking structures. This can lead to increased competition, lower transaction costs, and the development of financial solutions tailored to the diverse needs of the population.

Challenges and Considerations:

Implementing a decentralized currency system poses significant technical, regulatory, and adoption challenges. Ensuring the stability of the currency, protecting against cyber threats, and achieving widespread acceptance and use among the populace and businesses are critical considerations that need to be addressed.

Conclusion:

The decentralization of currency under Savaism represents a radical reimagining of monetary policy, aiming to create a more equitable, transparent, and stable financial system. The Federal bank and centralized currency system has been a nuisance on the financial system for too long now, but by leveraging blockchain technology to distribute financial power we can reduce central authority's influence. This reform seeks to align monetary practices with Savaism's broader goals of democratization, empowerment, and economic resilience.

Principle 8: Introduction of a GDP-Backed Stable Coin:

Central to Savaism's financial innovation is the introduction of a stable coin tied to the nation's GDP, designed to maintain a steady inflation rate of 1.5%. This digital currency, supported by blockchain technology, offers a decentralized and stable medium of exchange that reflects the real economic output and growth.

Key Features and Implications:

- GDP Linkage: By pegging the stable coin's value to the Gross Domestic Product (GDP), its value directly correlates with the country's economic health and performance. This linkage aims to ensure that the currency's purchasing power is grounded in tangible economic activity, making it a reliable store of value and unit of account.

- Controlled Inflation: Setting the inflation target at 1.5% strikes a balance between preventing deflation, which can hinder economic growth by encouraging hoarding of currency, and runaway inflation, which erodes purchasing power. This controlled inflation rate is designed to encourage spending and investment in a balanced and sustainable manner.

- Decentralized Currency Management: Utilizing blockchain technology for the stable coin's issuance and management decentralizes control over the monetary system. This minimizes the risk of political or economic manipulation, ensuring that currency policy is transparent and based on pre-defined rules rather than discretionary central bank policies.

- Not only would a GDP-backed stable coin be the most stable currency, but it could also become the world's reserve currency. Being the most stable currency tied directly to the largest economy in the world means other countries would trust and use it for international trade. Its stability would make it the go-to currency, replacing less reliable options and giving the global market something they could count on.

- Enhanced Economic Stability: A stable coin with a predictable inflation rate and backed by GDP can contribute to greater economic stability. It provides a hedge against the volatility associated with traditional fiat currencies and the speculative swings of unbacked cryptocurrencies.

- The real power of this stable coin comes from the transparency it provides. Because its value is tied to the actual economy—specifically the products and services we buy—it becomes clear when prices go up whether corporations are raising them unfairly. They can no longer blame inflation like they often do now. If the economy is stable, but prices are rising, people will know the corporations are responsible. This would force companies to think twice before unfairly hiking prices, as they would have to face public backlash. It gives the people more control and holds corporations accountable in a way that's never been possible before.

Challenges and Considerations:

The implementation of a GDP-backed stable coin involves complex considerations around the measurement and reporting of GDP, the technological infrastructure required for a blockchain-based currency, and the transition from existing monetary systems. Achieving widespread acceptance and integration into the global financial system are also key challenges.

Conclusion:

The creation of a GDP-backed stable coin with a set unchangeable inflation rate embodies Savaism's forward-thinking approach to monetary policy. This initiative aims to foster a stable, equitable, and resilient economy by aligning currency value with actual economic activity and growth. By leveraging the advantages of blockchain technology and decentralization, this stable coin promises to offer a secure, transparent, and efficient means of exchange that supports Savaism's broader economic and social goals.

Principle 9: Prohibition on Corporate Ownership of Residential Property

A distinctive policy within Savaism is the prohibition of corporate ownership of residentially zoned property, coupled with an emphasis on increasing residential zoning. This measure is designed to combat speculative real estate practices and ensure that housing remains accessible and affordable for individuals and families, aligning with the broader objectives of creating a more equitable and community-focused society.

Key Features and Implications:

- Combatting Speculation and Inflation: By preventing corporations from purchasing residential properties, this policy directly addresses the issue of speculative buying, which often leads to inflated housing prices and shortages. This approach ensures that homes serve as living spaces for people rather than investment vehicles for profit.

- Promotion of Affordable Housing: Increasing the zoning for residential properties encourages the development of more housing units, contributing to a greater supply that can meet the demand. This helps to stabilize or even reduce housing costs, making homeownership and renting more accessible to a broader segment of the population.

- Strengthening Communities: Restricting corporate ownership in residential areas supports the development of stable, cohesive communities. Homeownership is linked to numerous positive outcomes, including increased civic participation and better social and economic conditions. This policy fosters environments where residents have a long-term stake in their neighborhood's wellbeing.

- Encouraging Sustainable Development: With a focus on expanding residential zoning, Savaism also opens the door to integrating sustainable and environmentally friendly practices into new housing developments. This can lead to more green spaces, energy-efficient buildings, and community-oriented designs that enhance quality of life.

Challenges and Considerations:

The implementation of such a policy requires careful planning and enforcement to navigate potential resistance from real estate developers and corporations. It also necessitates a comprehensive strategy that addresses the diverse housing needs of the population, including affordable rental options and support for low-income families. It will also be important to create a legal distinction between private residential property and corporate residential property. As it stands "residential zoning" is a blanket statement applying to everything from apartments to homes. There will need to be a change in zoning laws to make this distinction between the purpose of the residential property in order to better protect the real estate.

Conclusion:

The prohibition of corporate ownership of residentially zoned property, alongside efforts to increase residential zoning, represents a commitment to putting the needs and well-being of individuals and communities at the forefront of housing policy. By tackling speculative practices and promoting the development of affordable and sustainable housing, Savaism aims to create a more equitable, stable, and cohesive society where everyone has access to safe and affordable homes.

Principle 10: Restructuring Government Financial Oversight

Savaism calls for the dismantling of the Internal Revenue Service (IRS) and the Federal Reserve System (Fed), aiming to radically reform the nation's financial infrastructure. This bold move seeks to eliminate centralized control over monetary policy and taxation, replacing them with systems that are more decentralized, transparent, and aligned with Savaism's principles of equity and direct democracy.

Key Features and Implications:

- Decentralization of Financial Authority: The abolition of the Fed signifies a shift towards a decentralized monetary system, possibly based on blockchain technology or other forms of digital currency that do not require central oversight. This approach aims to prevent the manipulation of currency and interest rates by a central authority, promoting economic stability and fairness.

- Simplification of Taxation: Eliminating the IRS is part of a broader move to simplify the tax system, likely replacing it with the Fair Tax policy mentioned earlier. This would involve a more straightforward tax mechanism that reduces bureaucratic overhead, compliance complexity, and the scope for evasion and loopholes.

- Under Savaism the US would benefit more highly from a treasury than a federal bank. This more accurately reflects the beliefs behind Savaism removing banks and bureaucracy. The IRS would also become near obsolete. With the implementation of the fair tax act there would be no need for a centralized Internal Revenue Service.

- Rather than having two entities responsible for one bureaucratic process Savaism proposes the idea of having more decentralized and technologically advanced systems. Rather than having a IRS and the Fed Savaism proposes having several different administrations, for example a taxation administration, a transparent treasury, an internal accounting administration, a foreign trade administration, a currency accountability administration, and more. Each of these would be more specialized and efficient. They would have more ability to make affective change within their specified field while less ability to reek havoc on the economy as a whole.

Challenges and Considerations:

The proposition to abolish the IRS and Fed faces significant challenges, not least in how to effectively transition to new systems without disrupting economic stability. It requires quality execution in the creation of the alternative structures for monetary policy and taxation that retain public confidence and international credibility.

Conclusion:

The abolition of the IRS and Fed under Savaism is a transformative goal that seeks to reconfigure the landscape of financial governance and economic policy. By advocating for efficient, simplified, non bureaucratic systems of monetary control and taxation, Savaism aims to create a more equitable and transparent economic foundation. This radical reform underscores a commitment to dismantling concentrated financial power and fostering a society where economic mechanisms are directly accountable to the people they serve.

Principle 11: Corporate Reorganization into A-Corp

A-Corp (noun): A type of corporation operating under principles of Savaism, where income is tied to the median employee wage, capped at 100 times that amount, and all profits are classified as personal income. A-Corps cannot trade stocks, issue dividends, or purchase residential property, with a structure focused on reinvestment and equitable compensation.

This reorganization promotes ethical reinvestment, discourages wealth hoarding, and limits income disparity.

Corporate Reorganization into A-Corp: Transitioning Corporations into a New Fair Form of Company

Under the economic model of Savaism, corporations are urged to transition into a more fair and equitable form known as A-Corp. These companies are designed to foster a more inclusive and just distribution of wealth by adhering to strict operating principles that ensure reinvestment and equitable pay practices.

The fundamental premise of A-Corps is that wealth should circulate throughout society, rather than being hoarded by a few at the top. This vision addresses the widening income disparity seen in both capitalism and socialism, but does so without heavy-handed government intervention.

Key Features of A-Corps

1. Income Capping and Correlated Income Ratios:
One of the key features of an A-Corp is the capping of earnings at 100 times the median income. This means that the highest-paid individual—including the CEO—within the corporation cannot earn more than 100 times the income of the average employee. To ensure fairness, A-Corps employ statistical methods such as outlier detection, exclusion, and trimmed means to accurately calculate the median, thus avoiding any manipulation of figures. 82% of wealth went to 1% of people in 2017. If we could turn that figure on its head then we could quadruple the average income. The income cap does this by incentivizing higher pay rather than government set minimum wages. The idea is to incentivize higher wages by tying it directly to the owner's income. This allows for a free market while still maintaining the middle class.

This model still incentivizes GDP growth because there remains the potential to become wealthy. For example, Elon Musk wouldn't necessarily be a billionaire, but he would still make a significant amount of money each year. The average employee at Tesla makes $105,000 annually. Without raising salaries, Elon would still personally earn $10.5 million a year. If he were incentivized to quadruple the salaries as described above, he could make $40 million a year. However, to achieve this, he would need to pay his employees $400,000 annually. Under this model, wealth would naturally begin to flow back into the middle class without penalizing ambition.

This system ensures a more equitable pay structure, discouraging the massive wage gaps that often plague traditional corporations. By aligning compensation with the company's overall financial health and the average employee's income, A-Corps aim to create a more harmonious and balanced workforce.

2. Legal Classification of Profits as Income:
A-Corps must classify any profits pulled from the company—whether as dividends, owner's draw, or other payouts—as personal income, making it subject to the income cap. This measure reinforces Savaism's commitment to preventing excessive wealth accumulation and promoting fair contribution to public resources.

3. No Stock Trading or Dividends:
In an effort to curb speculative behavior that prioritizes short-term gains over long-term sustainability, A-Corps are prohibited from trading stocks on public exchanges. This encourages businesses to focus on reinvestment, growth, and the welfare of employees rather than pandering to shareholders or market speculation. Dividends, which often lead

to wealth hoarding, are also eliminated, reinforcing the principle that profits should flow back into the business or to the workforce.

Benefits and Impacts of A-Corps

1. Encouraging Reinvestment:
By eliminating excessive profits and stock trading, A-Corps encourage reinvestment in the business itself. This could take the form of improved worker compensation, enhanced employee benefits, or capital investments that foster long-term growth and innovation. In the absence of high dividend payouts and speculative trading, wealth is continually cycled back into the company and its workforce.

2. Discouraging Wealth Hoarding:
The income cap and the classification of profits as taxable income act as deterrents against wealth hoarding. High earners are incentivized to reinvest in their business or support the economic well-being of their employees, rather than extracting large sums for personal gain. This model aims to diminish the growing income inequality seen in traditional corporatism, promoting a healthier, more equitable economic system.

3. Creating a More Equitable Corporate Structure:
The governance model of an A-Corp emphasizes fairness, sustainability, and collective well-being. It enforces a culture

where employees share in the company's success through better wages and improved benefits. Decision-making in these corporations tends to be more democratic, reflecting the interests of the wider workforce rather than just executives or shareholders.

Conclusion

A-Corps represent a bold and necessary rethinking of corporate structure under the economic philosophy of Savaism. They prioritize reinvestment, equitable pay, and sustainable growth, offering a new path for businesses that want to align with the principles of fairness and shared prosperity. Through measures such as income capping, reinvestment of profits, and prohibition of public stock trading, A-Corps aim to create a more just and sustainable economy for the future.

Sources:

1. BBC. (2018, January 19). What is Tesla's full self-driving technology? BBC News. https://www.bbc.com/news/business-42745853

2. PayScale. (n.d.). Tesla Motors salaries. PayScale. https://www.payscale.com/research/US/Employer=Tesla_Motors/Salary

4

Practicality

Historically this kind of reformation has called for revolution. Savaism is a new, unknown, untested economic model, and like any economic model it is not without flaw. There will be scrutiny and criticism and it is welcome. This idea is not to be taken without workshopping. Unfortunately the current leaders of this nation don't share my sentiments for change, and when I say leaders I don't mean politicians, I mean the 1%, or the 0.001%. The only people who hold the power to make change are the only people who stand nothing to gain from changing. They are the same people who stand everything to lose from changing and while they still benefit from Savaism, they stand to lose a lot from the switch to Savaism. Therefore this switch will require strategic moves.

Step 1: Create Awareness

The first step in making Savaism a reality begins with raising awareness. If people truly understood how broken the current system is, they wouldn't stand for it. As Henry Ford once said, "It is well enough that people of the nation do not understand our banking and monetary system, for if they did, I believe there would be a revolution before tomorrow morning." The truth is, much of the dysfunction we experience today—whether it's unaffordable healthcare, rising housing prices, or stagnant wages—isn't accidental. It's the result of a system carefully designed to benefit a tiny fraction of the population, while leaving everyone else behind.

People are struggling not because there's a lack of wealth, but because that wealth is concentrated in the hands of a few. The current system thrives on this inequality, keeping the public distracted, divided, and unaware of the extent to which they're being exploited. But what if people started to wake up to the reality? What if they began to question why the majority of the wealth they create ends up in the pockets of the ultra-wealthy?

How to Spark Change:

1. Start with Knowledge: Change begins with understanding. By learning about how the corporatist system functions—how monopolies, tax

loopholes, and political lobbying keep wealth concentrated at the top—you arm yourself with the tools to start conversations that matter. The more you know, the more you can help others see the flaws in the system and why change is needed.

2. Use Historical Examples: Throughout history, moments of crisis have revealed the true nature of financial systems. The Great Depression, the 2008 financial crash—these were moments when the cracks in the system became too large to ignore. When people see the parallels between these events and the current state of the world, they begin to understand that the system we live under is not built to last.

3. Relating to Everyday Life: Nothing hits harder than real-life stories. Rising rent, healthcare costs that make survival a financial burden, the inability to buy a home—these are issues almost everyone can relate to. When you start talking about how these problems are a direct result of the system being rigged, others will start to connect the dots. It's not about isolated issues; it's

about a system that's failing the majority while enriching the few.

4. Share the Message: Whether it's through social media, a blog, or a podcast, sharing what you know is key. People who are frustrated with the system need to know that they aren't alone, and that there's an alternative. Savaism offers a new path, one that prioritizes fairness, sustainability, and prosperity for all. By creating content, you're spreading a message that could inspire others to join the conversation.

5. Start Conversations: Awareness leads to dialogue, and dialogue leads to action. By sparking conversations with friends, family, and colleagues, you create a ripple effect. The more people start to question the current system, the more momentum builds for change. It's through these discussions that movements grow, and real, lasting change begins.

The first step toward Savaism is simply opening people's eyes. When enough people understand the truth about the system they live under, the demand for change will be unstoppable. Awareness is the foundation of any revolution, and once that awareness spreads, the possibility for transformation grows exponentially.

This is not just about ideas; it's about giving people the knowledge and the voice to demand something better.

Step 2: Create The A-Corp

Once awareness spreads, the next step in bringing Savaism to life is advocating for the creation of the A-Corp. New legislation would need to be introduced to create the A-Corp. this corporation type alone isn't enough. The plan also requires legislation allowing businesses to have the option to reorganize into an A-Corp as an alternative to declaring bankruptcy. Imagine for a moment if struggling businesses had the option to reorganize themselves into A-Corps rather than bankruptcy, where corporate vultures typically circle. The A-Corp could offer a lifeline to businesses and their employees, keeping them afloat while also aligning their operations with a new, fairer economic model. This requires pushing for real political change.

How to Move This Forward:

1. Advocate for the A-Corp Model: The first step is making sure people understand what the A-Corp is and how it can transform the economic landscape. This involves lobbying for the creation of laws that establish the A-Corp as a legitimate option for companies on the brink of bankruptcy. Lobbying may have negative connotations, but if Savaism is going to win, it will have to play by their rules. Mobilizing support

for the A-Corp means engaging politicians, business leaders, and the public to explain why this model is necessary for a more sustainable and equitable future.

2. Support Savaist Political Campaigns: For this kind of reform to happen, we need representatives in office who are committed to the principles of Savaism. Imagine donating to political candidates who are dedicated to pushing these ideas forward—people who are willing to fight for the creation of the A-Corp and other Savaist policies. Grassroots campaigns and crowdfunding efforts can play a huge role here, helping to elect politicians who are not yet bought by corporate interests.

3. Push for A-Corp Legislation: Change begins with the right laws in place. Getting laws passed that allow businesses to reorganize as A-Corps during bankruptcy would give struggling companies a second chance while also ensuring they adopt Savaist principles. This would involve proposing legislation at the local, state, and federal levels that enables businesses to convert

into A-Corps instead of collapsing under debt. It's not just about saving businesses; it's about saving them in a way that benefits everyone involved—employees, communities, and society as a whole.

4. Engage with Activists and Legal Experts: Legal experts and activists who specialize in corporate law and bankruptcy reforms will be critical in drafting and advocating for this kind of legislation. They can help shape policies that align with Savaism, ensuring that the A-Corp isn't just a theoretical model, but a practical, legally-recognized alternative for businesses across the country.

The creation of the A-Corp is more than just a legal formality; it represents the shift away from a system that prioritizes short-term profits and shareholder value to one that serves the long-term well-being of society. This new business model could be a game-changer for companies, giving them a chance to rebuild while aligning with Savaist principles. The key to this shift is advocating for the necessary legal and political changes, electing the right representatives, and rallying public support to make the A-Corp a reality.

In pushing for this change, we aren't just advocating for a new business structure—we are building the foundation for a more equitable economic system. The A-Corp can be the spark that ignites broader reform, showing the world that businesses can succeed without exploitation, and that wealth can be shared without sacrificing prosperity.

Step 3: Boycotts and Bank Runs

Once foundations for a better economy are in place, just like any construction, it's time to carefully dismantle the old. The wealthiest 1% will never willingly let the government take their money, so it's up to the people to show them it was never truly theirs to begin with. That means organizing bank runs, boycotting non A-Corps, and pulling stock investments from corporations that refuse to transition. Stir up enough disruption to force even the most unwavering corporatists to realize the system is broken. We voted these billionaires into power with our purchases. We will impeach them the same way.

The bankruptcy alternative wasn't just a financial aid package to struggling businesses but an opportunity to put the power of Savaism in the hands of the masses. If the A-Corp alternative exists then boycotts and bank runs will force the billionaires into submission.

But this needs to be done strategically—not in a way that leads to widespread economic collapse. We don't want another Great Depression, and we don't want to see mass unemployment or a plunge in GDP. The goal isn't to bring the country to its knees but to force each major NASDAQ corporation into the A-Corp reorganization. That means selectively shutting down banks and carefully bankrupting corporations one by one, not triggering a systemic crash.

1. Targeted Pressure on Key Players: Start with the most influential corporations—those whose collapse or reorganization will send the strongest message. Focus on the big names that symbolize corporate excess and exploitation, and force them to adapt. As each corporation falls, others will realize they're next if they don't make the switch.

2. Sustainability Over Shock: The intention isn't chaos for chaos' sake. The transition must be sustainable. If too many businesses fail all at once, we risk undermining the very economy we're trying to rebuild. Every step should be calculated, aiming for reform and stability rather than total collapse.

3. Public Buy-In and Awareness: Inform the public about why these boycotts and actions are necessary. The goal is to create a groundswell of support so that the movement isn't seen as anarchic, but as a deliberate step toward a fairer system. Without public awareness, the message will be lost, and people may panic. Transparency is key to ensuring that the public un-

derstands we're working toward a stable, equitable future—not a disaster.

4. Leverage Social and Digital Media: Use media strategically to expose the flaws in the current system and to highlight the progress of each corporation that transitions to an A-Corp. Public pressure can be amplified when people see tangible results, especially when influential figures and everyday people alike support the cause.

This is how we make the transition to a better economy. It's about taking down the old system, not recklessly, but purposefully. By doing it this way, we avoid a nationwide collapse and still bring about the fundamental change that Savaism seeks.

Step 4: Final Legislation

Once the people have successfully eliminated the S-Corp, C-Corp, and LLC structures, the corporate influence over politics will fade, finally allowing room for real change. With the A-Corp model now dominating, we turn to the next phase: electing non-corrupt politicians who will carry forward the Savaist vision. These leaders will be responsible for passing the final pieces of legislation, ensuring that the areas left unaddressed by A-Corps—like residential property and non-profit sectors—are properly reformed.

There are still several Savaist principles that remain untouched by the A-Corp transformation, and these need to be addressed through legislative reforms:

1. One key area is prohibiting corporations from owning residential property. While A-Corps can drive corporate responsibility, the housing sector must remain a separate concern. We must pass laws to ensure residential properties stay in the hands of individuals, not corporate entities. This step will safeguard housing affordability and prevent the kind of corporate speculation that has driven prices up and pushed homeownership out of reach for many.

2. Another crucial reform is the restructuring of essential services. Sectors like healthcare, insurance, education, and pharmaceuticals must operate as non-profits, ensuring that profit motives don't compromise the well-being of the people. Final legislation will mandate that these critical services be provided at or near cost, making them accessible to all citizens, and ensuring that no corporation profits from the public's essential needs.

3. Additionally, we need to ensure the decentralization of currency and financial authority. While A-Corps prevent wealth hoarding, a stable decentralized currency system needs to be established. This will ensure long-term economic stability and fairness by reducing the influence of central banking systems. A GDP-backed stable coin would ensure economic growth is tied to real production, while keeping inflation—artificial or otherwise—in check.

4. Finally, the abolition of the IRS and Federal Reserve must become law. These institutions have long represented an overreach of government power in controlling wealth and economic movement. Savaism envisions a simplified and transparent financial over-

sight system, replacing the IRS and the Fed with decentralized, streamlined institutions that align with Savaist values of equity and accountability.

By electing leaders committed to these principles and passing the final pieces of legislation, we ensure that the Savaist model will be fully realized. It is not just about transforming corporations, but about reshaping the very structures of society to reflect fairness, sustainability, and shared prosperity. These reforms will complete the Savaist transition, creating an economy that serves everyone, not just the elite.

Step 5: Supply and Demand Shifts

Once the final legislative changes are in place, the economy will enter a period of transformation, but in the best way possible. The wealth that was once locked away at the top will begin to circulate freely, and as a result, supply and demand will shift in ways we haven't seen in generations. Prices will fluctuate for a time, markets will adjust, but this is all part of the healing process. The abundance of wealth flowing through society will reshape the economy for the better, lifting up those who were once left behind.

In this new era, the middle class will rise again—not just as a small segment of society, but as the bedrock of a fair and prosperous economy. The great divide between the wealthy few and the struggling many will shrink, and the kind of life people dream of will be within reach for everyone. Imagine a world where a gas station employee can afford a home, where no one is drowning in debt just to survive. You'll be able to work a fair job and actually build wealth, not just scrape by. The culture of debt will be a thing of the past, replaced by a system that rewards hard work and investment in the future.

Healthcare and education, once a source of financial ruin for so many, will become an afterthought—a small, manageable expense that no longer dominates people's lives or savings. You won't have to worry about medical bills piling up, insurance companies denying you care, or crippling student debt. Instead, healthcare and education will be something you receive as easily and affordably as any other basic need.

As this economic rebirth unfolds, retirement will no longer be a distant dream overshadowed by the fear of not having enough. Instead, people will retire with true financial security—knowing they can enjoy the fruits of their labor, free from the constant grind of making ends meet. Abundance will no longer be reserved for the privileged few but spread across society, allowing everyone to live with dignity, comfort, and peace of mind.

This is the future Savaism promises—a world where prosperity is shared, where the economy works for everyone, and where the dreams of the past become the reality of tomorrow. It's not just about fixing what's broken but building a new system where wealth flows freely, lifting everyone up and leaving no one behind. A future where the struggles of today are distant memories, replaced by a society that values people over profits and fairness over exploitation. The economy will not just recover; it will flourish, and with it, so will every person who lives within it.

www.ingramcontent.com/pod-product-compliance
Lightning Source LLC
LaVergne TN
LVHW042246070526
838201LV00089B/39